LISBON

APA PUBLICATIONS

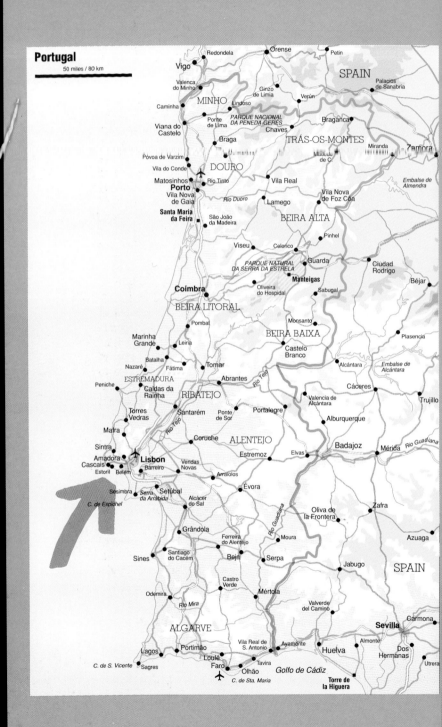

Portugal

50 miles / 80 km

Welcome!

Since the fall of the Salazar dictatorship in the Young Captains revolution of 1974 Lisbon has emerged as one of Europe's most dynamic capitals, as the upcoming *Expo 98* testifies. Yet much of the city's appeal for travellers lies in an older, more traditional side, where the spirit of the early discoverers and navigators still lingers and old-world elegance is never far away in the labyrinthine streets and alleyways of the Bairro Alto and the glorious azulejos adorning homes, restaurants, churches and metro stations.

In these pages Insight's specialist on Lisbon, Marion Kaplan, has designed three full-day and nine half-day itineraries to help visitors get the most out of Lisbon during a short stay. The former incorporate what she considers to be the most outstanding sights while the latter are designed to appeal to a range of different tastes. In addition, for those with time to venture further afield, she has included trips outside Lisbon – to Queluz and Byron's Sintra, to glamorous pousadas and into the beautiful countryside to the south. Supporting the itineraries are sections on history and culture, eating out, nightlife and practical information, including advice on hotels.

Marion Kaplan lived in Portugal for 12 years before writing this book, working as a photo-journalist for various publications. Her experiences and observations of a dynamic country on the move grew into a highly acclaimed book, *The Portuguese: The Land and Its People*, published by Penguin in 1992. In this book her aim has been to guide visitors not only to Lisbon's well-known attractions, but also to some of the delightful hidden corners that she has come to know and love over the years.

C O N T E N T S

Pages 2/3: seafront sun as Cascais

Excursions

For visitors with more time, two worthwhile excursions that can be made into the region around Lisbon.

Shopping, Eating Out & Nightlife

Calendar of Events

Practical Information

Maps

Index and Credits 86–90

Pages 8/9:
Tile picture of the
Praça do Comércio

HISTORY

Portugal was born in the northern town of Guimarães where, in 1109 or so, Teresa, daughter of the king of Castile and wife of Count Henry of Burgundy, gave birth to a son, Afonso Henriques. Her dowry was the green and hilly land between the Minho and Douro rivers, a place called Portucale.

Afonso Henriques was only five when his father died. Before he was 20 he had seized power from his regent mother and her lover. To the south, Moors – the word used to describe North African Muslims who had invaded in 711 – ruled the land. Afonso Henriques,

Castelo São Jorge, where Portugal began

forceful and ambitious, de-
termined to expand his realm.
In 1139, after a victory
against the Moors at a place
called Ourique, his troops
proclaimed him king. Leg-
end says that on the bat-
tlefield he had a vision of
Christ who foretold a glorious destiny for the Por-
tuguese people. Legends and
a sense of destiny were to ob-
sess the Portuguese for ever
after.

As you walk the broad
ramparts of São Jorge castle
in Lisbon, you are stepping
deep into the past. It is here
that the foundations of Portugal were laid. In 1147,
Dom Afonso Henriques, in a
massive assault aided by crusaders, giant catapults and

Afonso Henriques defeating the Moors

siege towers, conquered the castle and chased the Moors from their
citadel. Soon afterwards, the fortresses of Almada, Palmela and
Sintra were in his hands and, in 1158, with the fall of Alcácer do
Sal, the way to the south was open. By 1249, the Moors were gone
for good. The frontiers of Portugal have remained virtually the
same ever since.

Portugal has always been prized. Around the 15th century BC
Celts fought Iberians for possession of hilltop forts. Phoenicians
who came to trade around 1100BC were forced out by Carthagini-
ans and Greeks – who, in turn, were driven away by Roman armies

Royalty worship

between 400 and 200BC. (A Lusitanian rebel, Viriato, who resisted the Romans for years, is a national hero.) But by 60BC Lisbon, then known as Olisipo, was the Roman empire's western capital. Julius Caesar, finding the city pleasing, gave it a new name: Felicitas Julia.

The Romans eventually yielded to four tribes of Germanic barbarians: the Vandals, Visigoths, Alans and Swabians (or Suevi). The Roman legacy has endured in the network of roads, in cities like Conímbriga, in the notion of legal, civilised rule and in the Portuguese language itself, a Roman language with Latin roots. A power that would endure was also deeply rooted in Portuguese soil: Christianity. Strong enough to convert the Visigoths, whom the Moors overpowered in 711, Christianity grew to full vigour under Portugal's kings and queens.

Centuries of Dynasties

Between 1139, when the rule of Afonso Henriques began, and 1910, when the Portuguese monarchy ended with the exile of unlucky King Manuel II only two years after his father and older brother were assassinated, Portugal was ruled by only three hereditary dynasties, the Houses of Burgundy, Avis and Bragança. (A fourth, if you choose to include it – and most Portuguese don't – was the 60-year period after 1580 when the Spanish kings, Philip II, III and IV, ruled all Iberia.)

The accounts of chroniclers and historians of these varied dynasties are packed with gaudy tales of intrigue and foul deeds, murder and madness, of marriages that were often with Spain but sometimes with a handy uncle, aunt or niece, and of so many bastards that genealogists lost count. But most people acknowledge that there was also constructive rule that strengthened society and brought internal growth.

King Dinis, who reigned 1279–1325, exemplified the positive approach: he improved crops, planted forests, developed his fleet (under a Genoese admiral), advanced commerce by approving local fairs, designed new systems of administration and law and, to protect his realm from any threat from Castile, ordered the construction or refortification of castles up and down the land. He married a princess from Aragon, Isabel – so virtuous and chaste, so dedicated to God and the poor that she is ranked among the saints as Rainha Santa Isabel, the Holy Queen.

The practical Dom Dinis, a fine poet, won a much plainer title: *O Rei Lavrador*, the Farmer King. His farsighted thinking brought Lisbon new contacts. Despite the horror of plague, the Black Death

Henry the Navigator

of 1348 that decimated the population, Lisbon boomed. By the early 14th century as many as 450 ships sometimes lay at anchor in the Tejo river.

Of the illustrious characters in Portuguese history, Prince Henry the Navigator, born 1394, the third son of King João I and his English queen, Philippa, is renowned for sponsoring daring voyages of discoveries. In time they led to external expansion so astounding that, from the mid-15th century until the end of the 16th, Lisbon was the centre of trade and the wealthiest city in Europe.

Portugal's days of glory are long gone. The passage of time has seen some ironic turnabouts: Japan, whose entire foreign trade was dominated in the 16th century by Portuguese seapower, is now wooed by Portuguese industry. But much of what you see in Lisbon reflects its golden past. Museums record the city's colourful history, often in fascinating detail. In the Museu Nacional de Arte Antiga, among great paintings that include *The Adoration of Saint Vincent*, the 15th-century masterpiece by Nuno Gonçalves, you'll find Japanese *Namban* screens portraying the arrival of the 'barbarians of the south' in 1571. In the Museu da Marinha in Belém you can see how the Portuguese developed navigational aids, their exquisite maps, and their lively little caravel that was so easy to sail. And Belém's superb Jeronimos monastery was built by King Manuel I (called the Fortunate on account of the wealth he acquired) to celebrate Vasco da Gama's achievement in reaching India and opening a sea route from the west to the spices of the east.

There's true magnificence in constructions as

Lisbon harbour during the Great Earthquake

different as the massive monastery-palace at Mafra, built between 1717 and 1735 by 45,000 workmen to celebrate the birth of a child to King João V, or the same king's huge Lisbon Aqueduct of Free Waters, which survived the Great Earthquake of 1755. In the earthquake – it shook all Europe – some 30,000 of Lisbon's population (then 270,000) perished and much of Lisbon was destroyed by fire and flood. 'Nothing was left,' a witness wrote, 'but desolation and sorrow.'

Torre de Belém, typically Manueline

Yet Lisbon grew again in grace and stature under the guiding hand of the Marquês de Pombal, chief minister to the ineffective King José. The broad Praça do Comércio, the arch that opens to the *baixa pombalina*, the neat grid of streets still with their guild names in the lower city, are a part of Pombal's wide-ranging influence that included lasting social reforms.

In Portuguese culture, fine building is the dominant art. A heritage of empire, it lives on in castles and churches around the world; you'll see it in the variety of styles that adorn Lisbon, from medieval to Manueline, mannerist to neo-classical and post-modern.

You will sense a yearning for lost grandeur in every neighbourhood, see it in the faces of *lisboetas*, and hear it in the songs they sing and the jokes they make. In Lisbon's politics, monarchists still mourn the passing of the monarchy (everyone likes and respects the Duke of Bragança, a royal descendant). Except for a few reactionaries, no-one cares to recall the era of Dr António de Oliveira Salazar, the economics professor who admired fascism and ruled Portugal as a police state from 1932 for nearly 40 years. It was he, though, who cleverly kept Portugal out of World War II.

But perhaps most influential to the mood and spirit of the city is the fact that grand old Lisbon, which also escaped – largely through the brilliant tactics of the Duke of Wellington – the heavy tread of Napoleon Bonaparte's invading armies three times, has never experienced the agonies of war.

Symbol of modern Lisbon: Amoreiras Shopping Centre

Peaceful Revolution

Even the revolution Lisbon woke up to on 25 April, 1974, was peaceful. Carnations sprouted from the gun barrels of officers and troops (reacting primarily against the regime's war policies in Africa), a repressed people rejoiced and prime minister Marcelo Caetano, who had assumed Salazar's mantle when he became ill in 1968 (he died in 1970) was dispatched into exile. Exiles returned – a bright young socialist, Mário Soares, who went on to do two terms as Portugal's non-party President, was one of them – and, in uneven steps, democratic government was on its way. The soldiers were persuaded to stand back and, in 1987, after a series of collapsing governments, the Social Democrat party led by a youthful economist of modest origins, Aníbal Cavaco Silva, won a majority vote. Silva repeated his success in 1991, then was succeeded in 1995 by a socialist administration led by António Guterres. Soares was succeeded as president by Dr Jorge Sampais.

Historic perspective

Old hands in Lisbon have seen several changes in recent years. At the outskirts of the city, hypermarkets and factories have sprouted, along with hefty apartment blocks. Up the hill from Pombal's monument, you'll see the glass towers of Amoreiras, the shopping centre beloved by the city's youth. Many of these people are too young to know the pre-revolutionary Lisbon and take revolution's true prize, democracy, for granted, along with another benefit: now, they may kiss in public.

'Western Europe's poorest nation' is how Portugal has often been described in recent years, though since EC membership in 1986, there are new roads, modernised airports, an expanded and more efficient telephone system. Computers have arrived in government, industry, offices, and shops – though not quite everywhere. You'll still see tiny tailors' and cobblers' shops tucked

Youth of today

into big, bureaucratic buildings. You'll still find *lisboetas* musing on the past, talking, as if it were yesterday, about the horrors of Inquisition, suppressed in 1820. (The stunning new building of the national archives, Torre do Tombo, contains the records of over 36,000 cases for the years between 1540 and 1765.)

Lisbon's Pleasures

In the Graça neighbourhood you can still see on the second Sunday of Lent the solemn procession of the brotherhood of Santa Cruz dos Passos, which dates from 1634. Well, not that solemn: *lisboetas* love a gathering, and the occasion is as much social as religious. Someone will probably tell you the linguistic irony of Lisbon's largest cemetery: its name is Prazeres, which means pleasures.

Yet you'll soon discover that, though they have an enthusiasm for music, a delight in many art forms as well as the widespread *azulejos* (tiles), their language, so difficult for foreigners, is their true love. They are passionate about their numerous gifted writers, their classical novelists including Eça de Queiroz, the multi-character modern poet Fernando Pessoa and above all the 16th-century writer of the epic poem, *Os Lusíadas*, Luís de Camões.

You can take a coffee at A Brasileira with Pessoa beside you, lunch at the glittering Tavares Rico where the city's leading literary lights used to gather, dine at Leão d'Ouro, haunt of artists, or just have a snack at the Nicola, whose eminence derives from the acid poems extemporised by the brilliant Bocage. 'An honourable testament to civilisation', was how one *habitué* once described the Nicola. You might say that of all likeable, luminous Lisbon.

Historical Highlights

60BC Julius Caesar makes Olisipo the western capital of the Roman empire and calls it Felicitas Julia.

AD409 Germanic tribes invade. The Visigoths are the most enduring.

711 Moors from Africa occupy Iberia.

1147 King Afonso Henriques, with Crusaders, captures the Moors' citadel of São Jorge.

1173 St Vincent is proclaimed Lisbon's patron saint.

1249 King Afonso III transfers Portugal's capital from Coimbra to Lisbon.

1290 King Dinis founds a university, later moved to Coimbra.

1348 Plague – the Black Death – ravages Lisbon.

1373 Anglo-Portuguese Alliance is signed, and later confirmed by the 1386 Treaty of Windsor (unbroken to this day).

1415 Ceuta, on the coast of North Africa, is taken by a Portuguese force which includes Prince Henry the Navigator.

1487 Bartolomeu Dias rounds the Cape of Good Hope.

1494 Treaty of Tordesillas: Portugal and Spain divide the world.

1497–8 Vasco da Gama opens a sea route to India.

1500 Pedro Alvares Cabral lands in Brazil.

1531 Holy Inquisition is introduced.

1580 Lisbon falls under Spanish rule until 1640.

1661 England's Charles II marries Catherine of Bragança.

1706–50 Reign of King João V; Mafra monastery is built.

1755 The Great Earthquake devastates Lisbon.

1777 Maria I becomes queen; Pombal is dismissed; Lisbon gets street lighting.

1807–10 Napoleon's forces invade three times; Royal family sails to Brazil; Duke of Wellington's 'lines of Torres Vedras' save Lisbon from assault.

1834 Religious orders dissolved, church property seized, Maria II becomes queen, aged 15, marries Ferdinand of Saxe-Coburg-Gotha.

1856 The first railway line opens in Lisbon.

1908 King Carlos and the Crown Prince are shot dead in Lisbon.

1910 Monarchy is overthrown and King Manuel is exiled.

1926 Military coup overthrows Democratic government.

1928 General Carmona, as President, appoints Dr António de Oliveira Salazar finance minister; by 1932, he is the prime minister and rules Portugal as a police state until 1968.

1939–45 World War II: Portugal remains neutral. The oil millionaire Calouste Gulbenkian lives in Lisbon; he bequeathes his art and fortune to Portugal.

1966 Suspension bridge over the Tagus (Tejo) river opens.

1968 Salazar becomes ill (dies in 1970); Marcelo Caetano becomes prime minister.

1974 Young Captains' Revolution restores democracy to Portugal; Armed Forces Movement governs until 1976.

1975 Private banks and insurance companies are nationalised; monopolies and estates taken over by employees.

1976 A minimum salary of 3,300$00 is decreed; new constitution upholds socialism and democracy; General Ramalho Eanes is elected president.

1986 Portugal and Spain join EC. Mário Soares, three times socialist prime minister, elected non-Party president (and re-elected in 1991).

1987 Social Democrats win majority in National Assembly, and begin liberalisation of economy.

1988 Fire destroys most of Lisbon's Chiado area.

1989 Unemployment is below 6 percent; property restored to former owners; revised constitution opens way to privatisation and a free market.

1995 New socialist administration.

1998 Expo 98 comes to Lisbon.

Lisbon

0.5 miles / 800 m

BENFICA

Estrada de Benfica

Avenida do Uruguai

COLEGIO
MILITAR

DAMAIA

ALTO D
MOINI

CALHARIZ

Avenida General Norton de Matos

Rua C.Michaelis de Vasconcelos

Sintra

Cruz d
Pedra

PARQUE

Palácio
Fronteira

Forte de
Monsanto

SETE RIO

BAIRRO DA
BOA VISTA

FLORESTAL

CARNAXIDE

Aqueduto das
Águas Livres

DE MONSANTO

Auto Estrada do Oeste

Auto Estrada Viaduto Duarte Pacheco

Av. de Ceuta

Estrada dos Marcos

CASELAS

Estrada de Queluz

Estrada do Alvito

Cascais, Estoril

Avenida da Ponte

CARAMAO

ALCÂNTARA

Avenida das Descobertas

Av. de Ilha da Madeira

Casalinho da Ajuda

Rua Maria Pia

Rua Sampaio Bruno

Ajuda
Palace

Jardim
Botanico

Rua Cruzeiro

ESTRE

Calçada da Ajuda

Avenida de Ceuta

TAPADA DAS
NECISSIDADES

Igreja da
Memorial

Calçada da Tapada

L. de
Alcântara

C. das Necessidades

RESTELO

Avenida de Rostelo

Avenida Infante

Archeology &
Ethnology
Museum

Calçada do Galvão

BELÉM

Coach
Museum

Rua Jau

Avenida da Ponte

Gulbenkian
Planetarium

C.das Necessidades

Avenida R.de

Jeronimos
Monas-
tery

SANTO
AMARO

Rua de Cascais

Maritime
Museum

R.V.Portuense

Avenida Vinte e

Centro
Cultural

Praça do
Imério

Praça Alfonso
de Albuquerque

Rua da Junqueira

Avenida da India

Torre de
Belém

Monument of the
Discoveries

Ponte
25 Abril

Avenida da India

Rio Tejo

TELHEIRAS

CAMPO
GRANDE

Aeroporto
Portela de
Sacavém

Av. Padre Cruz

Al. d.L. de Torres

Avenida General Norton de Matos

Avenida Marechal Craveiro Lopes

CALVANAS

CAMPO
GRANDE

Avenida do Brasil

Rotunda
do
Aeroporto

Av. M.G. da Costa

TERESINHAS

Av. A.G. Coutinho

Av. Cidade do Porto

CIDADE
UNIVERSITÁRIA

City
Museum

ALVALADE

ALVALADE

Avenida Almirante Gago Coutinho

Az. das Teresinhas

Av. Luz Laranjeiras

Avenida dos Combatentes

Av. Prof. G Pinto

Av. da Igreja

Av. Rio de Janeiro

LARANJEIRAS

Avenida das Forças Armadas

ENTRE
CAMPOS

Avenida Estados Unidos da América

Av. Álvaro Pais

ROMA

SETE RÍOS

ENTRE
CAMPOS

CAMPO
PEQUENO

Av. F.M. Contreiras

Avenida Calouste Gulbenkian

Av. José Malhoa PALHAVÃ

Pr. de
Espanha

Avenida de Berna

CAMPO PEQUENO

Avenida João XXI

AREEIRO

Palácio
Galveias

Areeiro

CHELAS

C. de Outubro

Avenida da República

Av. A.J.de Almeida

Calouste
Gulbenkian
Museum

S.SEBASTIÃO

Av. António Augusto Aguiar

Av. Duque de Ávila

ALAMEDA

Fonte
Monumental

Av. Almir. Reis

R. B.de Sabrosa

Estrada da Chelas

SALDANHA

SALDANHA

Saldanha

AMPOLIDE

R. Marquês da Fronteira

Rua Castilho

Estufa
Fria

Estufa
Quente

PICOAS

R. P.de Melo

ARROIOS

Rua Morais Soares

ALTO DE
SÃO JOAO

Rua Gualdim Pais

Rua de Campolide

PARQUE

PARQUE
EDUARDO VII

ESTEFÂNIA

R. Gomes Freire

R. Jacinta Marto

Av. Almirante Reis

Av. Mouzinho de Albuquerque

E.D.Pacheco

Shopping
Centre
Amoreiras

Av. R.J.A.D.Aguiar

Marquês
de Pombal

Pr. Marquês
de Pombal

ROTUNDA

ANJOS

Av. General Roçadas

R.Dom João V

MOREIRAS

Largo do
Rato

Rua Alex.
Herculano

Rua do Salitre

Avenida da Liberdade

INTENDENTE

Rua da Penha

De Azulejos
(Museum)

RATO

Jardim
Botânico

B.LOPES

Madre de
Deus
(Church)

Saraiva

Jardim da
Estrêla

Rua de S.Bento

Rua Escola Politecnica

Restaura-
dores

AVENIDA

SOCORRO

GRAÇA

R.dos Sapadores

R.d.V.do Operário

CAMINHOS
DE FERRO

XABREGAS

ica
êla

Calç. da Estrêla

Rua da Lapa

RESTAURADORES

Estação
do Rossio

ROSSIO

S.Jorge
Castle

Santa
Engrácia

R. de Santa Apolónia

Avenida Infante D. Henrique

BAIRRO
ALTO

Calç. do Combro

Rua Aurea

São
Vicente

LA PA

Av. D Carlos I

Rua D. Luis I

BAIXA

Rua do Alecrim

ALFAMA

Artillery
Museum

Estação
Santa Apolónia

Antique Art
Museum

Avenida Vinte e Quatro de Julho

Sé
Cathedral

Praça do
Comércio

Av. Ribeira das Naus

Rio Tejo

Estação
Cais do Sodre

Terminal
Fluvial

Ferry to Cacilhas ⤶

Day itiner...

$\mathbf{O}$ld Lisbon, rooted on the northern bank of the River Tagus (or Tejo), packs most of its attractions into two compact and easily walkable areas: the city centre and Belém, 8km (5 miles) towards the river mouth and the Atlantic. Lisbon is often described as the city on seven hills. Though you can't count seven, you'll see immediately that, from the Baixa in the middle, the city rises steeply to east and west. You don't have to climb. There's transport up, and you can walk down. Since these hills are to me the essential Lisbon, I have made them the basis of my itineraries for your first two days – with Belém and the riverside for your third day. After that, you might try some of the half-day trips I suggest, or the full-day outings if you have time.

Street names are usually well marked on pretty tiles. Many of the pavements are cobbled, so be sure to wear comfortable shoes.

Spot the tram

You don't need a car for any of the itineraries I suggest within Lisbon, but for out-of-town trips it could be handy. You'll find city transport pretty good – except during the rush hours (8.30–9.30am and 5–7pm). Cheap tourist passes for the buses and trams – *eléctricos* – are available from the kiosk right under the Eiffel-designed Santa Justa elevator in the Baixa.

If you intend visiting several museums and taking public transport, then the Lisboa Card (main office off the Rossio in Rua Jardim do Regedor) is very useful. Taxis are inexpensive and also useful. But if you like walking, you're sure to like Lisbon.

São Jorge Castle and Alfama

From Praça do Comércio rising east to the Sé (Cathedral), to São Jorge castle, church of São Vicente de Fora, the national pantheon, the Thieves' Fair (Tuesday and Saturday only) and medieval Alfama. Lunch (or tea) at the castle, dine in Alfama, and watch the sunset from Graça.

One good reason for starting your first day in Lisbon in the riverside **Praça do Comércio** is to get your bearings, for all Lisbon sprawls up and around this low-lying focal point. This great square is also called Terreiro do Paço, the place of the palace. Though the Great Earthquake of 1755 levelled the palace, many *lisboetas* cling affectionately to the old name even today. There's even another name, Black Horse Square, though the horse, with King José astride, is actually a bronze-weathered green and a Lusitanian, a breed which is a rich brown or grey, never black. The irony may take your mind off another: that this handsome square, lapped gently

by the waters of the Tejo, with arcaded ministry buildings to the east, and fine buildings (with a post office) to the west, is merely a traffic-rimmed car park.

The walk up to São Jorge is easy. Even if you go gently, and linger in places, it shouldn't take you much more than an

Boat's view of the Praça de Comércio

Lisbon Cathedral

hour. If you prefer, you can take a tram, No 28, from Rua da Conceição, the third east-west street in the Baixa grid from the square; the ride (to the Largo das Portas do Sol) takes barely 10 minutes.

A few steps back from the Largo brings you to the Travessa de São Jorge from where it's only a short stretch up to the castle. If you're coming by car, turn in at Travessa de São Jorge, follow the drive on up, follow 'Castelo' signs and find a car-parking space inside the castle gates. The same tram, No 28, will take you further up to the church of **São Vicente de Fora**, which is included in the walking route. You'll see more if you walk instead of ride, but the route is the same.

From Rua da Conceição, heading east, you'll see the Madalena church to your right, and up a short way, in a little Largo off Rua de Santo António da Sé, a church, the **Museu Antoniano** (10am–1pm; 2–6pm, closed Monday, free on Sunday) with a fun tile picture of St Anthony preaching to fish, and a charming statue all honouring Lisbon's best-beloved saint, St Anthony of Padua (1195–1231), who was born in the Alfama district.

A few steps up from here you'll see in front of you the bulk of the **Cathedral**, or Sé, its central rose window softening the outline of the two battlemented side towers. The monumental Romanesque

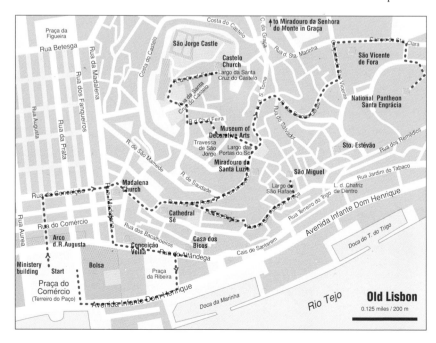

Old Lisbon

0.125 miles / 200 m

By the tiles at Santa Luzia

façade and Gothic cloisters are its most notable features. The dark interior contains the remains of patron saint São Vicente and the tomb of the 13th-century King Afonso IV, notorious in Portuguese history for having bloodily ended the love affair between his heir, Pedro, and a Galician lady, Inês, by having Inês murdered. When Pedro eventually succeeded to the throne, he had Inês exhumed and made his court pay homage to her corpse. Look out for Espaço Oiko, opposite, an art-space in a converted stable, with cobbles and troughs still in place.

Virtually beside the cathedral, as you carry on up, in Rua Augusto Rosa, are a couple of antique shops: Galeria da Sé, Nártice and Murteira. They display fine furniture as well as predictable sacred art. You are now in Rua do Limoeiro (lemon tree). Here, in 1385, when the Burgundy dynasty collapsed, a popular revolt, Europe's first revolution, brought Dom João I of the House of Avis to the throne. His marriage to the English Philippa produced several sons, among them Prince Henry the Navigator.

On your right is a small balustraded garden beside the modest church of **Santa Luzia** frequented by card-playing gents and lovers. From here there is a grand view down to Alfama and, in blue-and-white *azulejos* (tiles) on the church wall, the Terreiro do Paço the way it used to be. Told in tiles, too, is the story of Martim Moniz, close friend to King Afonso Henrique: in the 1147 assault on São Jorge he held open a castle gateway as Moors hacked at him with their swords.

To your left off your route you'll see a narrow street, Travessa de São Jorge, which broadens and leads up, in an easy stroll, to the castle. If you've started out late in the morning, then take the turning and head on up. You could lunch there, inside the castle walls, or close by – see my suggestions below.

With time in hand, carry on along the tram route – you'll find liquid refreshment in the **Largo das Portas de Sol** where a shining statue of São Vicente, ship and ravens in hand, stands conspicuously at the approach. In this pleasant Largo, too, is the **Museum** of **Decorative Arts of the Fundação Ricardo Espírito Santo** (10am–5pm, closed Monday) with collections of furniture, porcelain, paintings and fine silverware.

This area is vibrant with life and colour. Trams rattle by and the twisting byways of Alfama weave all around. But if you wander into the enchanting alleys and beckoning *becos* (lanes) be sure you've got valuables well stowed. This district is renowned for its *ratos* – rats, the local word for thieving youngsters.

On round the bend, the tram route divides. Follow the right-hand fork down the hill into the narrowing and winding Rua das Escolas Gerais. Where the line starts to ascend and divides into two again, the church of **São Vicente de Fora** (daily 9am–1pm and 3–5.30pm) looms large to your right, its Mannerist facade ornamented with a variety of decidedly animated statues: *de fora*, meaning outside, reflects the fact that the church once stood outside the city walls.

View from the castle

Inside the church is a splendid sacristy and, along echoing cloisters whose 18th-century tiles depict the much-loved fables of La Fontaine, the tombs of Bragança kings and queens (9am–1pm and 3–5.30pm). If you find the atmosphere gloomy now, there was a time, not so long ago, when the Bragança bodies, encased in glass, lay exposed to view.

Outside the church, turn sharp right so that you are walking beside it and go under a tall archway to the Campo de Santa Clara. Any day but Tuesday or Saturday when the **Feira da Ladra** (Thieves' Fair) is held, it's a peaceful place and you can bear right calmly, take the first turning on your right and follow the road as it zigzags briefly to the pale stone domed **national pantheon of Santa Engrácia**. An imposing baroque building, begun in 1682, it took nearly 300 years to complete and houses national figures and presidents. The latest to be honoured was the freedom fighter General Humberto Delgado, murdered by Salazar's secret police in 1965.

On Tuesday and Saturday all peace and tranquillity depart from the Campo de Santo Clara. The twice-weekly Thieves' Fair is a large cheerful market where you can buy practically anything, from new and worn clothing or fish, fruit and vegetables to boots or books. Come to browse through a splendid selection of pure junk and occasional gems.

Return (by tram or foot) to the access to **São Jorge castle**, and lunch. If it's market day and you fancy a picnic, buy bread, fruit and cheese, head back the way you came, downhill, turn right at the Travessa de São Jorge just after Largo das Portas de Sol, have a beer, perhaps, at A Tasquinha, the café with the bright umbrellas on your way up, and relax on the broad ramparts of the castle (entry is free). You'll find cafés, bars, ice-cream, as well as souvenirs and

postcards by the castle gates.

If you want to treat yourself to something special, there is a classy restaurant, the handsomely tiled **Casa do Leão** (tel: 887 59 62), inside the castle walls. It is part of the *pousada* group of state-run hotels and one of its specialities is *ameijoas na cataplana*, steamed clams. Lunch hours are 12.30–3pm.

Over the years São Jorge castle has been a citadel and stronghold, a prison and a theatre. Now, despite battlements and ramparts, it's a peaceful garden with tall trees and fountains, peacocks and swans, where elderly *Lisboetas* play dominoes and families bring their children for an afternoon out. The view, down to the city and across the Tejo, is truly spectacular. Sao Jorge actually has two gates – the outer arched and the inner less grand – as well as two inner areas: the skirt of the castle, with walkways, play area and mini zoo, views and the restaurant, and over a moat, the castle itself with stairs up to the battlements.

Once you've seen everything you want, turn left after exiting the inner gate and head up the narrow street of little old ladies to reach the peaceful Largo da Santa Cruz do Castelo, the former artisans quarter.

Alfama street

Your afternoon should be devoted to a gentle exploration of Alfama. You'll probably want to detour from the route I suggest, attracted by tantalising glimpses of pretty houses, elegant balconies, gaudy tiles, pot-plants and fluttering laundry. Alfama is a labyrinth but, as long as you remember that the river is downhill and the castle uphill, you can easily find your way out.

I suggest you return to the tram route below, but instead of carrying on down to the front of the cathedral, take the road behind it, the slanting Rua do

Barão, which leads into Rua de São João de Praça. This leads straight into the Largo de São Rafael and, bearing left down a narrow lane, to the **Largo de São Miguel**. The church is one of the oldest in Lisbon and much admired for its interior decoration (though it's not always open).

In this charming little square, to the left as you arrive, you'll see a restaurant called **Malmequer Bemmequer**, meaning 'He loves me, he loves me not' (its logo is two daisies). The food here is good and inexpensive and you might like to return here for dinner (tel: 887 65 35). Since taxi drivers dislike the narrow lanes of Alfama, remember the way from the cathedral. If you're here in June, when Alfama celebrates the *festas* of the popular saints – for virtually the whole month – the neighbourhood is festooned with paper decorations and explodes with song and music.

With São Miguel's location lodged in your mind, walk back past the Cathedral, following Rua de Santo António da Sé. Turn left onto Rua Madalena. From here, it's just a short walk down to the Rua da Alfândega where, on the left, you'll see the Manueline (late Gothic) doorway of the old Conceição Velha church. The street leads into the Rua dos Bacalheiros. The building on your left whose entire facade is a mass of studs is the **Casa dos Bicos**. Of 16th-century origin, the building now houses the offices of the Discoveries Commission.

You're virtually beside the river at this point in the itinerary. Bearing right you'll soon come reach the Praça do Comércio and familiar territory. It may look a little different at this time of the day, though. As the afternoon lengthens into evening commuters crowd toward the ferry terminal and kissing couples gather on the river terrace. The old Terreiro do Paço is a favourite trysting place among Lisbon's young.

A last thought for your first day in the city: there's no better sunset view of old Lisbon, the castle and Alfama at dusk than from the neighbouring Graça hilltop. If you go by cab, ask for the **miradouro da Senhora do Monte** in Graça; if by tram, No 28 brings you to the Largo da Graça. Take the first turning to your left and keep going – only 300m (984ft) or so – to the hilltop. A few steps downhill, at 39, Calçada do Monte, you'll find the **Albergaria Senhora do Monte**. A very pleasant place to stay, it also has a pleasant rooftop terrace and bar where you can watch sunset or moonrise, with a glass in hand.

26

DAY 2

A day in lively central Lisbon, its bustling streets and shops; ride Eiffel's elevator to ruined Carmo, see kiosks with character, the Jesuit São Roque; taste port and have a seafood lunch; walk the warren of the Bairro Alto and shop in the Chiado; dine out and stay out to listen to 'fado'.

Like the Praça do Comércio the **Rossio**, with the Avenida da Liberdade to the north and the Baixa to the south, has more than one name. For the Rossio it's Praça de Dom Pedro IV, after the king whose statue tops a pillar in the middle of the square. He has a fine view of flowersellers, shoeshines, shops, cafés, a taxi rank, the Valentim do Carvalho music store and, almost next to it at the western corner across from the Dona Maria II theatre, a public telephone office where, from 7am–11pm (Sunday and holidays 9am–11pm) you can telephone home. It is not unusual for places to have more than one name: Rua Garret, the prime shopping street, for instance, is also known as the Chiado, the name for the surrounding area damaged during the 1988 fire, now almost all reconstructed.

A significant part of central Lisbon, the **Baixa**, meaning low, is a simple chessboard of parallel streets, several pedestrianised. It is flat, small and easily walkable. The Baixa, between the Rossio and the Praça do Comércio, is the grid of 17th-century neoclassic buildings designed by the Marquês de Pombal after the 1755 Great Earthquake. He had crafts in mind, reflected in such street names as the Rua da Prata and Rua do Ouro for silver and goldsmiths. Some are still there, along

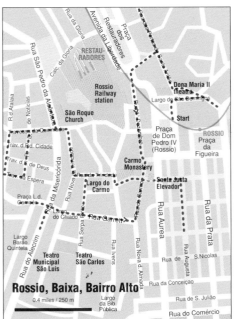

Rossio, Baixa, Bairro Alto
0.4 miles / 250 m

Rossio flowersellers

with other shops, elderly or entirely modern. But central Lisbon has much to see around the Rossio and the Baixa, too.

You could start with an invigorating coffee at the **Nicola**, elegantly-fronted haunt of the poet Bocage just behind the square's west side On Rua 1 Dezembro, then head behind the Dona Maria II theatre to Rua de Barros Queiros which, bearing left, brings you to the Largo de São Domingos. Once, this area was the headquarters of the Inquisition. Now you'll see a quiet church, a clothing store, a greengrocer and three of Lisbon's numerous jewellery stores. Are you about to celebrate a birthday or an anniversary? Lisbon's gold is always 19¼ carats.

On the north side of the theatre you come to the Rua das Portas de Santo Antão, newly cobbled for pedestrians only. It's a street redolent of old Lisbon: on your left at No 17 is silversmith **Barreto e Gonçalves**, at No 25 **Gambrinus**, a pricy restaurant favoured by financiers. On your right at No 32 **Guedes, Silva e Guedes** stocks traditional knobs and knockers as well as plainer hardware. On your left is a stylish grocery, **Manteigaria Londrina**, selling port, cheeses, smoked ham and sausage, and next to it, at No 57, the **Frutaria Bristol** (the English are longtime allies of Portugal).

Street life

A little further on your right you'll see the **Coliseu** variety theatre and, just after it, the **Sociedade de Geografia de Lisboa**. In the society's lobby is a handsome 19th-century painting of Vasco da Gama being received in India – somewhat coolly as his gifts were paltry – by the ruling Zamorim. (If you are keen to see the great hall, Sala Portugal, designed by Eiffel, free tours are offered on Monday, Wednesday and Friday at 11am and 3pm.) Just beyond is a popular seafood restaurant, the **Sol e Mar**, but today I have other ideas for you.

Turn around and come back the short stretch to the street on your right marked Rua do Jardim do Regador. Before you head into it, look left and, at No 58, you'll see the almost anonymous exterior of the **Casa do Alentejo**. Enter, climb the stairs, and you'll find a riot of interior styling: Moorish courtyards, Art Deco flourishes, magnificently tiled banquet hall and restaurant with massed panels of vivid *azulejos*. Once a palace belonging to the counts of Alverca, it has since been the 1920s informal club and the regional house of Alentejanos. Its restaurant serves hearty Alentejo dishes for lunch and dinner every day but Sunday – but again I'm not proposing you lunch here today.

Lisbon is crammed with restaurants. If you now walk along the Rua Jardim do Regador you'll see on your left the good, cheap and cheerful **Sol Dourado**, its window stacked with seafood, which is another option to keep in mind for days to come. The Lisboa Card office is on your right. Beyond, on the left, is a shop, **Regional Madeira**, specialising in Madeira's lovely embroidered tablecloths. In front now is the Praça dos Restauradores, a big plaza that stretches on your right to the broad, tree-lined Avenida da Liberdade. Just steps to your right is a kiosk where you can book tickets for Lisbon events. Across the road and a few metres to the right past the Hotel Avenida Palace and the mock-Manueline Rossio railway station is the main **Turismo** office. If you haven't already been there, they'll provide you with a city map, find you accommodation and answer queries.

Luvaria Ulisses, for gloves

Heading towards the Baixa now, past Rossio station, carry straight on into the pedestrian Rua 1 Dezembro where, at No 93–7, there is **Leão d'Ouro**, a restaurant which was virtually the club of Lisbon's artists during the 19th century. It has a cool, arcaded interior. A food store, **Celeiro**, smells good at No 81–83, its big windows temptingly filled with gourmet food and snacks such as shrimp rissoles; different aromas emanate from No 29, a perfumery appealingly named **Oh! La!-La!** In a row on your right beyond it are shoe shops galore – Anusca, Tania, Roma, A Deusa, Sapataria Presidente, Flavia and, in front of you at the corner where Rua do Carmo begins, Charles.

The sloping Rua do Carmo is lined with attractive shops devoted to shoes, books or clothes. The tiniest glove shop you ever saw, **Luvaria Ulisses** (legend says that Ulysses founded Lisbon), is squeezed

The Santa Justa elevator (foreground) and Carmo ruins

in at No 87A; a jeweller's, **Joalharia do Carmo**, occupies 87B. The street has been largely redeveloped following the Chiado fire, up to where it meets Rua Garrett, which I will come to later. Meanwhile drop down to the Eiffel-designed **Santa Justa elevator**. Access to it is down the steps at Rua de Santa Justa. As you walk down you'll see a ticket office where you can buy your visitor's pass for Lisbon transport.

The ascent is brief but, quite suddenly, Lisbon looks different. It isn't just the grand view across rooftops, which can be enjoyed from the café on the top. Head inland on the walkway and you emerge into the graceful **Largo do Carmo** (not always so quiet: in April 1974 the prime minister and conservative leaders took refuge in the barracks here as crowds grew outside). Immediately to your

The Carmo monastery

right are the roofless ruins of the **Carmo monastery**, victim of the 1755 Earthquake. The monastery was founded in the 14th century by Nuno Alvares Pereira, an army commander who became a monk, the closest friend of Dom João I. Now, elegiac and still lovely, it's a modest **archaeological museum** (10am–1pm and 2–5pm, closed Sunday and holidays) where concerts are sometimes performed under the stars.

From the right corner of the square the Rua da Trindade bears right into the Rua Nova da Trindade. On your right is the **Livraria Barateira** which sells new and second-hand books (in English and other languages). Just beyond, you'll see the yellow awning of the **Cervejaria Trindade**, a very popular and colourful restaurant (*cervejaria* means it's also a beerhall) where the prawns are delicious, the waiters friendly and the ambience relaxed. This is my suggestion for lunch. First, however, providing you haven't lingered too long in shops and it's still reasonably early, you might look around the area a little.

Just ahead is the **Largo de Trindade Coelho** (also called São Roque), its colourful kiosks rather more conspicuous than both the Misericórdia building in one corner (a wealthy charity founded some 500 years ago and funded from the national lottery) and, tied to Misericórdia historically, the Jesuit **São Roque church** in front of you (8.30am–5pm; holidays 8.30am–1pm). The latter's interior – it's cool inside and you can sit down – compensates for its dull exterior with a huge painted ceiling and eight richly decorated chapels; the most opulent a 1750 masterpiece dedicated to St John the Baptist, incorporating lapis lazuli, agate, porphyry, alabaster, amethyst, jade and different marbles, ordered from Rome by King João V. You might prefer the less lavish 17th-century geometric tiles at the back of the church. (For a small fee you can also see the collection of European religious art in the church **museum**, entered from the church.)

If you'd like a light tawny port as an apéritif head up the road beside São Roque. At No 45 in the Rua São Pedro da Alcântara is the Port Wine Institute's **Solar do Vinho do Porto** (10am–midnight, closed Sunday and holidays). Its deep armchairs are soothingly comfortable, and the barman can offer you a port (though nothing else) from a selection of around 6,000. If you don't care for port, relax for a moment in the gardens opposite where there's yet another grand view of old Lisbon.

Rich interior at São Roque

Returning to the Cervejaria Trindade for lunch, note as you leave the Solar do Vinho the bright yellow **funicular tram** across the road; it has plied the Rua da Glória for a century. If your time is short, it could take you quickly down to the Restauradores. To your right, those narrow parallel streets are in the Bairro Alto (upper town). You could explore them briefly after lunch and, if you like, return tonight.

More than anywhere in Lisbon, the Bairro Alto leads a double life. Walk the streets of the Bairro by day and you'll see well-proportioned houses with handsome balconies and many flowerpots. Families live here, many without bathrooms, often over tiny workshops,

Café in Largo do Chiado with a bronze of poet Fernando Pessoa

cramped grocery stories, printing establishments, shops selling books or antiques, and tiny family *tascas* serving cheap lunches. At night, in the glow of the street lamps, the Bairro Alto assumes a different personality with its numerous smoky *tabernas*, bars, restaurants and *fado* houses, discos and *boîtes*.

For a daylight impression of the Bairro, you could walk up the Travessa da Queimada from the Largo de Trindade Coelho (São Roque) to where it meets the Rua da Atalaia. (At this corner on the left is a popular restaurant, the **Bota Alta**, serving excellent Portuguese food which is a good option for dinner.) This afternoon, however, I'm proposing that you carry on down to the Chiado so, for the moment, you might just walk a few steps back down Queimada, take a right at the Rua da Barroca, left at Travessa do Poço da Cidade, left at any of the next three small streets, to bring you back to the Travessa da Queimada and the Largo da Trindade.

From here walk back down Rua Nova da Trindade but, at the Rua da Trindade, instead of turning toward the Carmo monastery, carry on down through Largo Rafael Bordalo Pinheiro into Rua Serpa Pinto and down into Rua Garret.

Rua Garret – the Chiado – has several elegant clothes and dé-

Ceramics for sale

cor shops. Starting from the bottom, classical Lisbon is found in the **Casa Pereira,** selling teas, coffees and chocolate at No 38, and, further uphill, at No 50, the grand **Ouriversaria Aliança**, specialising in silver. Across the road and up you'll see a bookshop, **Livraria Bertrand**, and **A de Sousa** for fabrics and lace, on the corner after the church. Up the Chiado, No 18 in the Largo do Chiado, is the handsome porcelain shop of **Vista Alegre**, founded 1824. Just before it is the café **A Brasileira**. You could take a coffee at an outside table, the poet **Fernando Pessoa** beside you in bronze.

Two other literary idols are close by – **Luís de Camões** has an imposing statue just ahead in the Largo de Camões and, if you walk a short distance down Rua do Alecrim, left from here, a statue of the 19th-century novelist **Eça de Queiroz** gazes upon a naked muse in the Largo Barão Quintela. Just below, at the corner, is the **Sant'Anna** tile shop, founded in 1741, which maintains a selection of superb ceramics and *azulejos*. This street, too, is noted for antiques.

How much energy you have left probably depends on how much you like walking – and shopping. If you don't, Lisbon's cheerful cafés offer refreshment and breathing space and you might like to pass the rest of the afternoon watching the world go by from a table in the Baixa. To walk there from Sant'Anna go back up to the Largo do Camões, down the Rua Garret and into the Rua do Carmo and down the steps, right, at Rua Santa Justa. Off the broad, traffic-free Rua Augusta, second to your right, are several other areas good for walking, with street cafés.

For this evening I suggest dinner (see *Eating Out* for my recommendations) followed by some *fado*, Portugal's traditional music. *Fado* singers start late, usually not before 10pm. If you want dinner with *fado* (see the section on *Nightlife*) remember that the food is not cheap and the songs are often depressingly soulful. That said, many *fadistas* have a huge following among the Portuguese and *fado* should be experienced at least once during your stay in Lisbon. An easy way to hear as much, or as little, as you want is to dine relaxedly first, then go to a bar where there's *fado vadio*, that is, where anyone can get up and sing. Along and around Rua do Diário de Notícias are several such bars, often apparently nameless. At the corner of Rua Diário de Notícias and Travessa da Espera (a dark doorway) is a bar once famous as the haunt of the *fadista* Deolinda; page 72 has details of other *fado* bars. Wherever you find yourself, order an *aguardente velha*, a classy brandy, or a cheaper, stronger *bagaceira*, sit back and absorb the music and the spirit that are both pure Portugal.

DAY 3

Riverside Lisbon

A day by the Tejo (Tagus), starting in the east with the 'azulejos' at the tile museum, then going west to the city market, and on to beautiful Belém, the Jerónimos monastery and the coach and marine museums. A riverside lunch, tea, dinner and disco. If you want to follow my recommendation and lunch at Já Sei!, it is sensible to book (Tel: 301 59 69) before you set off. The restaurant is closed Monday.

Boats on the Tejo

Marvellous museums and grand sights extend in a row rimming the river. Start east of the city in Xabregas (bus No 59 from the Praça da Figueira until it leaves the main highway, then walk under the railway arch) at the **Museu Nacional do Azulejo** (10am–6pm and 2–5pm; closed Monday), in the magnificent setting of the Madre de Deus convent founded in 1509 by Dona Leonor, widow of Dom João II. (An unloving wife, she founded the Misericórdia charity organisation, which is still going strong today.) The church, which has an ornate and typically twisted Manueline portal, glitters with gilded baroque wood-

18th-century azulejos

work, splendid paintings and tiles, some Dutch. Tiles in the sacristy (18th century) were made in Lisbon's Rato factory. In the cloisters you'll see *azulejos* from five different centuries, showing the gradual changes in colour, style and taste, including florid tile panels, charming scenes of old Lisbon, art deco and modern.

Azulejos, sacred and secular, fanciful or plain, are a major Portuguese art. If you've travelled by train in Portugal you'll have noticed how they adorn every station. The display here is a grand summary of nationwide decoration. Don't miss it. The cafeteria is a pleasant oasis on a hot day.

A brisk walk (or buses 104 and 105) along the road, Cruz da Pedra, with the docks to your left, brings you to the little **Museu de Água** (Tuesday–Saturday 10am–12.30pm and 2–5pm), the Water Museum of EPAL, the water company. It won the Council of Europe's museum prize in 1990. To get there, look for Calçada dos Barbadinhos to your right and, a little further on (follow the signs up the hill), a village square opening to the museum's garden. Honouring Manuel da Maia, the engineer who built Lisbon's great Aqueduct of Free Waters in the 18th century, the museum was created from the 1880 Barbadinhas Pumping Station and still retains – its main attraction – an impressive machine room where four mighty steam engines rise through three floors in a colossal mechanism of iron, copper and wood. One engine operates by electricity so you can see it functioning. To walk the Great Aqueduct, see the half-day itinerary No 9 later in this book, where the route is described in some detail.

The **Museu Militar** (Tuesday to Saturday 10am–5pm) looms large

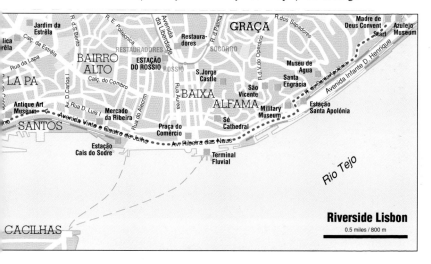

as you approach central Lisbon, with the main railway station, Santa Apolónia, to your left. (The distance between the tile and military museums is about 1½km/1 mile.) The archway under guard on the eastern side, topped by martial sculpture, is not for sightseers, though. The massive ochre-coloured building is military territory; entry to the museum is in the Largo da Arthilharia on the west side guarded by a suit of armour on the roof (who says the Portuguese military have no sense of humour?). Even if displays of weaponry don't enthral, there are some intriguing items such as the gadget invented especially to set in

Torre de Belém

place the statue of King José in the Praça do Comércio.

Here you might grab a cab or hop on a bus (No 17, 28 or 35) past the Praça do Comércio to the **Mercado da Ribeira**, Lisbon's main market, though it will be rather quieter now than early in the morning. On the way, you pass the Cais do Sodré station on the left, where electric trains leave for Cascais and points west, including Belém, and the traffic-encircled Praça Duque da Terceira on your right.

On next to **Belém**. Take the smart new No 15 tram or the No 14, 28 or 43 bus. Once there, distances are manageable on foot. You might like to lunch at the very pleasant riverside restaurant **Já Sei!** – reasonable prices for excellent food including delicious fresh

The Discoveries Monument, Belém

fish. (The name means 'I already know' or, more colloquially, 'got it!') If you haven't booked and it's high season, get there early. There's a glass-walled room for cool days, and a terrace. You will find it just to the west of the Discoveries Monument (reached by a pedestrian tunnel underneath the railway line if you find yourself inland of the line), with the Torre de Belém further west along the river. Leave the Belém village, monastery and nearby museums until after lunch. If you're driving to Belém, keep an eye open for the road access signs that let you through to the Torre and Monument and across the rail lines.

There's much to see at Belém, an area closely associated with the Age of Discoveries and which feels like a seaside town. It was from the river shore here in 1487 that Bartolomeu Dias set sail on the voyage that would take him round the Cape of Good Hope, opening the sea route to India. When he reported to King João II in December, 1488, Christopher Columbus was also at court, frustratedly seeking sponsorship for a voyage of his own. When Vasco da Gama sailed from the Tejo shore in 1497, it was a major expedition with two big square-rigged *naus*, one nimble caravel that had proved its worth on voyages down the African coast, and a store ship carrying provisions for three years. He spent 93 days at sea in a masterly feat of navigation that brought his fleet safely to the South African coast above what was to become Cape Town. From Malindi, the passage to India, the first by any European voyagers, took 26 days. The homeward voyage, hampered by rain, contrary winds and scurvy, was hard: when Vasco da Gama arrived in Lisbon in September 1499 he had lost two of his ships, two-thirds of his crew and his own beloved brother. The king – now Dom Manuel I – commemorated the voyage with the great Jerónimos monastery. Before a stone was laid, new fleets had already sailed for India. In 1500, the Portuguese also discovered Brazil.

Discoveries led to empire, wealth, exploitation, colonisation – all now in the past. Today Belém's exquisite buildings and museum displays celebrate navigational skills in general as much as the feats of Portugal's courageous mariners.

The **Torre de Belém** is a Manueline gem (reach it along the roadside, not the waterfront). The little tower, built by Francisco Arruda between 1515 and 1521, delights the eye with its setting on the very edge of the Tejo (though once it was on dry land), its perfectly-proportioned cupolas and the repeated theme of the Cross. Inside, you can peer into a dungeon and climb the tower, but its true charm, as its architect surely intended, is appreciated from the outside.

The **Discoveries Monument** (Padrão dos Descobrimentos) contains a museum devoted to different aspects of

By the sea at Belém

Mosteiro dos Jerónimos

the discoveries. The central theme of the displays changes from time to time. An elevator takes you to the top where there is a fine view of the Tejo, of Belém and, at the foot of the monument, a vast paved compass. The design of the huge monument, built during the Salazar regime, has never been admired, yet the carved stone figures of Prince Henry the Navigator and the explorers, mariners, traders and creative spirits he inspired are undoubtedly compelling. You might see, too, the scale of the sculpture emphasised by youngsters climbing among the figures.

The celestial sphere at the foot of the monument, a motif you may have seen at the tower, was adopted by King Manuel the Fortunate as his personal symbol. Thanks to wealth garnered from the spice trade and the profits made from exploration, Manuel was the richest king in Christendom who bestowed on himself grand titles; but he had been born in quite modest circumstances in Alcochete, just across the Tejo. The most eloquent legacy of his remarkable reign, in which small Portugal dominated far oceans, is Belém's **Mosteiro dos Jerónimos**, the Jerónimos monastery (10am–6.30pm, closed Monday).

The Manueline style – a l6th-century Portuguese adaptation of late Gothic – gives the monastery its striking individuality. First to work there was Diogo Boitac in about 1502; the monastery was completed some 70 years later. The entrance is through an elaborate portal peopled with stone figures (possibly including, on the central pillar, Henry the Navigator; as always, historians disagree). The interior is lofty and harmonious, with slender columns rising to a graceful vaulted roof. In the chancel are the tombs of Dom Manuel I and Dom João III and their queens (Manuel married three times: it is his second wife, mother of his 10 children, who lies in Belém); in the south transept is the tomb of poor foolish King Sebastião whose death in North Africa brought the Avis dynasty to an end. Though relatively plain, purity of line is emphasized by the elephants (symbols of power) that support the sarcophagi. Epic poet Luís de Camões and explorer Vasco da Gama are honoured by effigies. In the dramatically florid cloisters (separate entrance fee), you'll observe harmony of line and imaginative ornament (sometimes echoed in sound when modern orchestras hold concerts here).

The monastery extends almost seamlessly to the west, in more modern additions. There's a **Museu Nacional de Arqueologia e Etnologia**, with well-presented Roman and Etruscan ceramics, and next to it the **Museu da Marinha** (10am–6pm; closed Monday), with a separate section beyond the Calouste Gulbenkian Planetarium. You'll see model ships, busts of the great, furniture of the famous and the extraordinary, varied effects of empire – from Japan, from Goa in India, from Macau (where Portugal's flag still flies). A showpiece is the little aircraft in which Gago Coutinho and Sacadura Cabral flew over

Relic of a grand tradition

the south Atlantic in 1922. If you can't encompass it all, don't miss the explorers' navigational instruments and their very beautiful maps.

To the west of the marine museum is the low square building of the new **Centro Cultural de Belém**. Opened at the beginning of 1992 during Portugal's presidency of the EC, its scale is rather dehumanising but its range of events and exhibitions is impressive. Roller-bladers have colonised its open spaces.

The row of houses fronting the green park and the river in the Rua Vieira Portuense (not obvious from the road, so approach from the park) are pure old Belém, tasteful and charming. Behind, in Rua de Belém, extending east from the monastery, are shops, houses and restaurants. Fancy some refreshment? Across the road at No 86 is the famous *pastelaria* **Pasteis de Belém** where, surrounded by elderly ladies and gentlemen, you can order tea and one of their delectable cream cakes, *pastel de nata*.

Detail from the Museu dos Coches

If you continue east you will pass in a few steps the pink palace that's now the official residence of the president of Portugal before reaching the **Museu Nacional dos Coches** (10am–5.30pm, closed Monday). The coaches themselves are a grand enough sight yet some *lisboetas* regret that this place became a museum at all. It was designed as a school for the royal horses but became a museum at the wish of Dona Amélia, wife of King Carlos. Fans of the lovely Lusitanian horse believe that, with its painted ceiling and fine gallery, it could have been a setting as grand and famous for Portugal's elegant Escola Portuguesa de Arte Equestre as the famous Vienna school is for Lippizaners. Some consolation for those keen on horses is the ceremonial Changing of the Guard in which horses parade and helmeted bands play, held in front of the palace on the third Sunday of the month.

How fast have you been touring? How much do you want to see? The **Palácio Nacional da Ajuda** is lkm (half a mile) away, up the steep hill of the Calçada da Ajuda at the corner of the coach museum (take any bus). One of those massive Lisbon buildings never quite completed, it has a permanent exhibition about the monarchy and, quite often, excellent displays in a separate gallery. The last part of the approach is through cool and shady gardens with fine views. On the downhill route you'll see almost immediately the high walls that enclose one of Lisbon's botanical gardens. Cut across west along the Rua do Jardim Botânico, left and down the Calçada do Galvão and, in 200m (650ft) or so, you'll see to your left the impressive dome of the **Memória church**. You'll have discovered that the influence of the Marquês de Pombal, baneful and beneficial, lies heavily on Lisbon. Here, at last, he came to rest: in a small chapel, in a small box, are all that remains of Pombal.

Searching for bait

Towards evening have a comforting drink in a neighbourhood bar, wander back to the river and watch Belém glow in the setting sun. Take the evening slowly. Have dinner, perhaps at the very reasonably priced restaurant, **O Rafael**, at 106 Rua de Belém, or one of the cheap and chirpy restaurants in Rua Vieira Portuense (**Montenegro** at No 44, **Cais de Belém** at No 64 or **O Alexandre** at No 84). Or, to watch the light fade over the river, you could go back to Ja Sei!. Want to be closer to the city centre? Try **Sua Excelência** at 40–42 Rua do Conde, well-liked for its good cooking and owner (Tel: 60 36 14). Energy restored, you can carry on, perhaps, to the **Kremlin** disco in Santos (No 1, Rua das Escadinhas da Praia) and, with the river running by, dance the night away.

There's a wide choice of places to go and things to do in and around Lisbon in just half a day. My suggestions are divided into morning, afternoon and evening trips. There's nothing to stop you switching some of these, or extending them. Where hours or events are fixed, I have said so.

Morning Itineraries

1. Palácio Nacional de Queluz

Lisbon's Versailles, the prettiest of palaces

Queluz is just west of Lisbon and easily accessible – by train from Rossio station to Queluz-Belas station, turn left, go down the steps into the town, under the old arches, and walk straight down for 800m (½ mile), or by car west along the motorway towards Cascais (stay in the right-hand lane, go slowly and take the inconspicuous turnoff for Sintra, then take the road signposted for Queluz and the palace, which appears almost immediately at your left).

The pink rococo **palace** at Queluz (10am–1pm and 2–5pm) was built between 1747 and 1752 for a son of King João V, Dom Pedro, by the Portuguese architect Vicente de Oliveira. Gardens and extensions, with echoes of Versailles, were designed by the Frenchman Jean-Baptiste Robillon. The palace became the favourite residence of Dom João VI and the gardens the pleasure of his virago of a wife, Carlotta Joaquina.

The gardens, trimmed parterre hedging in the formal style, with elegant pools and walkways, urns and statuary, are classic Portugal. Look out for the tiled watercourse. The palace's two storeys include a throne room, fine furniture, gorgeous ceilings, a gold-trimmed oval hall of mirrors, and the circular bedroom where King Pedro IV was born in 1798 and died of consumption at the age of

36. His short life was also complicated: the liberal victor in the War of Two Brothers against his absolutist brother Miguel, he had been Emperor of Brazil and king of Portugal and had abdicated both his titles. A man of constitutional principles and grand gestures, he bequeathed his heart to the city of Oporto in appreciation of the northerners' loyal support; the heart is kept in a church in Oporto to this day.

Queluz is a small town with its own character. There are several cafés (there's one across from the palace) or, for an understandably high price, you can lunch in style in the palace itself in the restaurant **Cozinha Velha** (tel: 435 02 32 to reserve). The former kitchens have been glamorously transformed and are managed by the national enterprise that runs the *pousadas*.

If you are here during August and September and want to see Queluz by night, it is worth checking at Queluz or with Sintra Turismo (tel: 435 00 39 or 923 11 57) to see if there are performances of the gorgeous summer spectacle **Noites de Queluz**. A fantasy of dance and music evocative of court life in the 18th century, the stunningly costumed shows (9.30pm) bring the palace and gardens enchantingly back to life.

Palácio Nacional de Queluz

A brief look at the highlights of Lisbon's finest art museums, including Gulbenkian's modern art centre.

The surfeit of culture in this option might appeal on a cool or rainy day. The museums are all within Lisbon (though too far apart for comfortable walking), and I've outlined some of the highlights so that you can savour their essence without trying to digest them whole. The feast, though, is rich and exciting.

The **Museu Nacional de Arte Antiga** (National Museum of Ancient Art 10am–6pm, closed Monday), in the Rua das Janelas Verdes, down near the river (bus No 27, 40, 49 or 60), is housed in a large and much remodelled 17th-century palace, with excellent displays and a cafeteria downstairs with a terrace overlooking the river.

The all-powerful Marquês de Pombal lived here for a time. The heart of the collection is its 15th- and 16th-century art, much of it religious. The Portuguese School includes such leading artists as Gregório Lopes. A number of paintings by grand international names are here, too, including Dürer's hypnotic *Saint Jerome*, Hieronymus Bosch's *The Temptation of Saint Anthony*, Cranach the Elder's *Salome*, and Breughel the Younger's *Beggars*. Velasquez is represented by a portrait of Mariana, wife of his patron King Philip IV, and Andrea del Sarto by a self-portrait.

From the Museu de Arte Antiga

Portugal's greatest masterpiece may also contain a self-portrait. The polyptych *Adoration of Saint Vincent*, six panels by Nuno Gonçalves, painted around 1467 as an altarpiece, vividly portrays some 60 figures – many, like Prince Henry the Navigator, seemingly familiar. It honours, in effect, the early discoverers. Among the faces is possibly Nuno Gonçalves himself up in the top left corner.

In a way, exploration is the theme of the intriguing Japanese *Namban* screens here which show the arrival in Japan of the Portuguese in 1571, the 'barbarians from the south' whose appearance the Japanese found alarming and odd. Another of the museum treasures is the *Monstrance of Belém* crafted by Gil Vicente in 1506 from Indian gold shipped back by Vasco

A Japanese 'Namban' screen

da Gama. He was, it's thought, the same Gil Vicente who is Portugal's greatest playwright.

The **Museu da Cidade** (City Museum), up and beyond the Avenida da Republica, sits calmly on the western side of the big traffic circle where Campo Grande disappears under the main east-west flyover. Take a cab, or a bus No 1, 36, 38, 44 or 45 up the Avenida. So discreet you might not see it at first, the museum (10am–1pm and 2–6pm, closed Monday and holidays) occupies the Palácio Pimenta, a delightful country residence with sunny rooms, big tiled kitchens and garden, that has survived the mesh of roads that now surround it. Here you will find encapsulated in great detail all of Lisbon's long and enthralling history, even – with appropriate shards and bones – pre-history.

The Romans are represented by stones from a theatre, funerary stones, and a sly sculptured satyr. You'll see the 1217 *foral* (city charter) of Dom Afonso II confirming the one conceded by King Afonso Henriques (note the paragraphs promising penalties for selling wine in the period reserved for the king). There's a memorable engraving of the moment in history (1662) when Catherine of Bragança departs Lisbon to marry England's Charles II. The growth of the city is portrayed in marvellous 16th-century drawings, in *azulejos* and in engravings of Lisbon before the Great Earthquake struck in 1755, and there's a large model of how it looked at the time. The earthquake, fire and tidal waves are dramatically rendered by several artists. The Inquisition is present in engravings of torture and a well-attended *auto da fé*, a burning. The designs for the aqueduct are also here.

There are appealing ceramics; fine lithographs by Manuel Luiz of costumes in Lisbon in the 1840s, alive with barking dogs and brush salesmen; appealing miniatures by Robert Batty in 1830; and wonderful water colours by George Atkinson (1838). Photos mark the proclamation of the Republic in 1910, and you are virtually back in modern times with Almada Negreiros' striking portrait of Fernando Pessoa, Portugal's most prominent modern poet.

To go from Campo Grande to the **Calouste Gulbenkian Museum** (winter: Tuesday–Sunday 10am–5pm, closed Monday; summer: Tues-

The Monstrance of Belém

day, Thursday, Friday and Sunday 10am–5pm, Wednesday and Saturday 2–7pm, closed Monday), located on the corner of Avenida da Berna in Praça da Espanha, you could take a cab, or bus No 31, 41 or 46 as far as the bullring at Campo Pequeno and then walk the short distance west down the Avenida da Berna. The building is low and modern, set in landscaped gardens. Downstairs, a cafeteria serves refreshments.

The art is the remarkable personal collection of one man, born in Istanbul of Armenian parents in 1869. Calouste Gulbenkian adored fine art and began collecting even before his deals in the oil industry gave him the nickname Mister Five Percent and immense wealth. Most of his collection he reserved for his own pleasure in his Paris home. In World War II he came to neutral Portugal and took up residence in Lisbon. He liked it here and, helped by a distinguished lawyer, set up a foundation. When he died in 1955 at the age of 86, he left his entire art collection to Portugal. His bequest founded the museum housing it (with concert halls and exhibition rooms), a symphony orchestra, ballet company, choral group and libraries galore. His wealth was poured into medicine, the social services, education, culture and the arts; through careful management, it is greater now than during his lifetime.

Gulbenkian had wide-ranging tastes. His collection here is divided broadly between Eastern and Western art and sub-divided into his particular enthusiasms, often repeating itself in several examples of the same thing. You are sure to like, as much as he did, the Egyptian bronze cats, though you may not share his passion for Greek coins. You will undoubtedly admire his Persian carpets and the Chinese and Japanese porcelain.

The Western art ranges from master painter to masterpiece. You'll see works by Rubens and Rembrandt, English artists such as Romney and Gainsborough, and French Impressionists including Renoir, Degas and Monet. Superb sculpture includes a grand *Diana* by Houdon and bronzes by Rodin. The collection includes 16th-century books, French fine furniture, furnishings and silver. Don't miss, in a separate room, René Lalique's Art Nouveau jewellery. Gulbenkian admired it so much that he acquired 169 pieces when he was still young and not particularly rich. Modern Portuguese art is not ignored by the Gulbenkian Foundation. Across the gardens is the separate **Centro de Arte Moderna** (same days, hours, and entry cost as the Gulbenkian museum) where a lively art scene is well represented. Particularly striking are the stellar works by the late Maria Helena Vieira da Silva, born in Lisbon in 1908, and the much younger and still very vigorous Paula Rego.

Has your own vigour begun to fade? Revive it on the spot with food and drink. You will get a tasty self-service meal in the Centro's restaurant.

3. The Gardens of Lisbon

Soothe the spirit on a sunny morning with a wander around a selection of Lisbon's loveliest gardens.

Lisbon flower lady

The **Jardim Botânico** (Monday–Friday 9am–7pm, weekends and holidays 10am–7pm) is hemmed in by buildings and you need to look carefully for the main gate at 58 Rua da Escola Politécnica. Access to the garden is down steps to the right of an imposing edifice that began life as the Jesuit Colégio dos Nobres and later served as the untechnical terrain of Lisbon University's Science Faculty. The botanical garden, a cool shady place founded in 1873, is rich in rare plants (over 2,500 species) from low shrubs to tall trees. The garden's design incorporates various biblical allusions. An avenue of different palms, for example, is said to symbolise the triumphal entry of Jesus of Nazareth into Jerusalem.

Tucked into an upper corner of the Parque Edouardo VII, named in honour of England's Edward VII who visited Lisbon in 1903, are two large and astonishing greenhouses, the **Estufa Fria** and **Estufa Quente** (cool and hot). The park (open daily 9am–5.30pm) stretches uphill from the Praça Marquês de Pombal, the big roundabout, also called Rotunda, at the top of the Avenida da Liberdade. The main entrance is from the west side

In the Estufa Fria

off Rua Castilho. On foot you can make your way in from the park's broad central walkway. Entering the Estufa Fria, under its canopy of slatted bamboo, is like wandering into a jungle where flowering plants, familiar and exotic, grow in such flourishing abundance that you cannot see round the bends in the path or along the purling stream at your feet. Water flows wherever you walk, in small fountains and waterfalls, rippling ponds and rivulets: on a hot day, nowhere in Lisbon is more cooling. Small bridges and the occasional statue punctuate the garden; benches are judiciously located. Where the Estufa Fria opens into the rather hotter Estufa Quente you suddenly enter a steamy valley of tall cliff, spiky cactus and ponds where wild birds shriek and flamingoes pose.

Back outside, you're within easy reach of a long cool drink at the Hotel Meridien or the Hotel Ritz Inter-Continental on the Rua do Castilho, or in one of the small cafés in the streets stretching uphill from them. Incidentally, the battlemented castle at the top of Rua do Castilho is a prison.

If you haven't run out of time, or want to see more of Lisbon's lovely gardens, try to fit in the **Parque do Monteiro-Mor** (Tuesday to Sunday 10am–6.30pm, closed Monday and holidays) at Lumiar, on the northern rim of the city, where superbly designed gardens in different styles embellish the **Museu do Traje** (costumes museum) and **Museu do Teatro** (theatre museum), both former palaces. I recommend you take a cab there and then the bus back (Nos 1, 7, 7B or 36).

Handier, smaller, and botanically unpretentious is the popular **Jardim da Estrela**, (daily 7am–midnight) beside the domed basilica built at the behest of Queen Maria I and where, in grandeur, she now lies.

In a Lisbon garden

As you follow the itineraries in this book you will come across a number of other gardens, including the 7 hectares (17 acres) of the Gulbenkian Foundation, the flowerpot-crammed yards of Alfama, grounds of palaces, and city squares. You are, however, unlikely to see carnations. A former mayor of Lisbon allegedly banned them from the city's gardens on account of his personal distaste for the flower. Nobody seems to miss them. Among Lisbon's small Edens and heavenly horticulture, nor will you.

4. Palácio da Fronteira

A grand house covered in weird and wonderful tiles

The Palácio da Fronteira (tour every morning at 11am; be there at 10.45am) is one of the finest and oldest (about 1670) aristocratic houses to be seen in Portugal today. Set back from the tall and ugly blocks of Lisbon suburbs, it's in the Largo São Domingos de Benfica, a short way beyond Sete Rios and the zoo. The No 46 bus will take you within easy walking distance. If you're driving, take the Sete Rios direction from the Praça de Espanha, and look for the Benfica sign. At Cruz de Pedra, a railway station, stay right and take the lane for Monsanto, then go under the rail bridge and bear right. You'll arrive at the gates of the terracotta-tinted palace in less than five minutes; there's parking outside.

In 1910 the Portuguese monarchy was swept away by republicanism and, in theory, titles were abolished. But if you visit and tour the magnificent 17th-century palace of the Marquês de Fronteira you may find you have the erudite and multilingual marquis as your guide. His ancestors built the palace; he lives there now, deeply immersed in its history and engaged in its conservation.

The palace, sometimes *quinta*, meaning manor house or property, is a marvellous evocation of many arts. The graceful house itself is fronted by Palladian loggias, with fine

Decorating the palace

formal gardens at the back beside a great water tank with elaborate balustraded walkway and set piece corners. On interior and exterior walls, on the tree-shaded terrace, you'll come across extraordinary, idiosyncratic tiles. Some of them are comic, others are startlingly rude.

Inside the house, you'll be shown the music room. Its tile-panelled walls depicting battle scenes of the restoration wars against Spain capture all the furore and horror of war in full swing: horses leaping and fuming, riders falling. They are in sharp contrast to scenes elsewhere (by a different artist) of gentle rusticity and piping farmers and the *trompe l'oeil* whimsy of an elegant hall in an apparently open door. On the terrace, artistry shifts again, from strong thematic statuary to tiles depicting angry-eyed cats and a trumpet-playing monkey. There's much to see, both classical art and vivid work by an unknown artist with a fantastic, even surreal, eye.

The conducted tour lasts until around noon. Expect to pay more than the normal museum price. Admission charges are 50 percent higher at weekends.

Lisbon's history is immured in old stone buildings; but these aren't the only structures worth attention. Equally intriguing from an architectural point of view are the turn-of-the century domestic townhouses, or the brash post-modernist edifices of architect Tomas Taveira. As you wander through old city streets you'll see door-ways, windows, balconies, arches, *azulejos* designed with an imaginative eye and placed with a decorative touch. It's hard to choose, but I'm listing here a few eyecatching buildings – odd, character-istic or distinguished – to look out for, beginning in the Rossio.

Prominent in the Restauradores is the mock-Manueline (late Gothic) **Rossio** station. Just south of the Rossio, through the Arco da Ban-deira, you'll find the **Animatógrafo do Rossio**, charming Art Nou-veau outside (and showing 'adult' movies inside). Proceeding up the Avenida da Liberdade with scarcely a pause, except a nod at the top in greeting to the Marquês do Pombal high on a pillar amid the circling traffic, and right to **28 Av Fontes Pereira de Melo**, you come to a virtuoso 1900s *palacete*, today the head office of the Lisbon Metro. Further on, in the Avenida da República (with better buildings though lacking the Avenida da Liberdade's pleas-ant walkways and greenery) you might stop for a coffee or tea at the **Pastelaria Versailles** at No 15, on your left and almost unno-ticeable from the outside. Founded in 1929, the tea-room with its mirrors, chandeliers, frescoes – and good tea and pastries – is both the most famous of Lisbon's tea-rooms and a social institution.

From here, take a cab up to **Largo da Graça**, in the neighbour-hood above Alfama. Grace, it means, and grace it has, in spite of dilapidation. On one side, the Villa Sousa's broad entrance was de-signed for coaches; the barracks on the other were originally built

This fine building now houses the Lisbon Metro headquarters

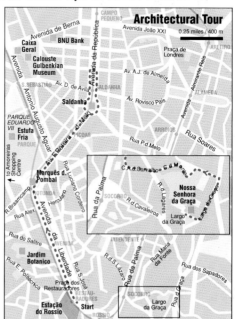

n the Graça district

as a monastery. Turn left from Rua da Graça into Calçada do Monte and, to walk down (shortish blocks but steep), take the left curve down the increasingly steep hill, turn right at the T-junction and sharp left into Calçada de Agostinho de Carvalho. At the bottom, turn right into the level Rua do Benformoso (signposted Rua do Terreirinho). In 250m (820ft) or so, past small unfashionable shops and the plain-faced street girls who linger in the doorways of a tawdry section at the end, you arrive in the Largo do Intendente, usually full of parked trucks. Beyond them on the left is the classically, colourfully tiled facade of the **Fábrica Cerâmica Viúva Lamego**, a long-established (1849) tile factory where you'll find a shop full of good Portuguese ceramics.

For a sharp contrast, turn left into the main Avenida Almirante Reis, grab a cab and head for **Amoreiras**, the gargantuan complex of post-modern towers and shopping centre (10 cinemas and several fast food restaurants) by the architect Tomás Taveira, built in 1985. You'll see more of his fanciful style in the BNU **Bank** on the Avenida da Berna between **Campo Pequeno**, the mock-Moorish bullring, and the discreet, modern **Gulbenkian Museum** (detailed in *Pick & Mix* itinerary 2).

Lisbon's latest notable building is the vast modern headquarters of the **Caixa Geral** savings bank at Praça de Espanha. Even here, in one of the world's biggest banks in size (250m/820ft façade, total area 207,000sq metres/51 acres) you'll notice the hint of a battlement. They like castles in Lisbon.

51

Afternoon Itineraries

6. Estoril, Cascais and the Guincho

Lisbon's prime resorts. Go by electric train from Cais do Sodré to Estoril and Cascais, and by car to the Guincho beaches.

With an identity, history, population, activity and atmosphere quite different from Lisbon, Estoril, Cascais and the Guincho form Lisbon's cherished resort area. It starts just over 20km (12 miles) west of Lisbon, and extends round the mouth of the Tejo and up the coast. It has beaches galore. Those on the estuary are often jam-packed in summer and neither water nor sand as clean as they should be, but the great ocean-washed beaches along the western Guincho, where winter winds can howl and breakers dash dramatically, are far less busy.

By train to Cascais

When conditions are just right, usually around September, surfers congregate. Leisure activities are plentiful all along the coast. You can play golf or tennis, go horse-riding, windsurf or sail (see Sport in *Practical Information*). The famous Estoril casino is here, if you like gambling. At the Autodromo on the Sintra road, you can watch Formula One car racing every September.

The coast is an easy drive on the new IC15/A5 motorway out of

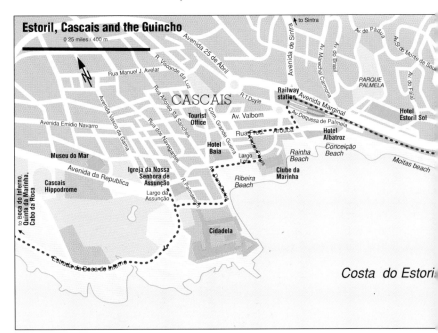

The beach at Cascais

Lisbon and, if you want to go to a Guincho beach or drive some way out of Cascais, it is worth hiring a car. For Estoril and Cascais, you could do what many residents do: take the train from Cais do Sodré to **Estoril**. The station is neatly located with a beach and the sea on one side and the Casino and its attractive gardens on the other. Crossing the Marginal into the **Casino gardens**, you'll notice a Tourist office in the lefthand corner where you can collect a map of the area. There are some attractive shops behind Turismo and in the arcade on the opposite side of the gardens. If it's not too early walk up on the parallel outer street for tea at the Palace – a real tea, elegantly served, in the dignified drawing room of the **Hotel Palácio**. In World War II the Estoril area acquired a glamorous reputation. Enjoying the breeze of neutral Portugal, German spies flocked to the Hotel Parque while English spies lodged at the grander Hotel Palácio. Graham Greene gave Lisbon espionage a literary lustre. There was also an exotic community of royal refugees which included the toppled King Umberto II of Italy, Carol II of Romania, a former king of Bulgaria, the Count of Paris, pretender to the French throne, and Don Juan, the father of the present king of Spain, Juan Carlos – who grew up in Estoril and remembers it affectionately. Gossip among these deposed royals was rife; it included scandals concerning the visiting Duke of Windsor.

The **Casino**, seen at its best from the non-garden side, opens at 3pm, but you will need a passport if you want to go in, and gamblers must be over 18 years old. You might like to check out the entertainment, or the slot machines (jackpots enticingly high), if you fancy returning later.

From Estoril, you can either take the train one more stop to the Cascais station, or follow the bank of the river on foot. The Circuito do Manutenção, the name of the boardwalk from Estoril to Cascais, is for pedestrians only, and is about 1km (½ mile)

Cabo da Roca (background) is Europe's most westerly point

long. You'll pass two big hotels – the Atlântico first, then the tall block of the Estoril Sol. In some ways bustling **Cascais** still thinks of itself as a village. The elegant Hotel Albatroz, superbly located between two pretty beaches, Rainha and Conceição, still has the look of the stylish mansion it once was. Much more than Estoril, Cascais focuses on the sea, a picture-postcard bay with bright fishermen's boats and a beach. Well placed though not particularly glamorous is the Hotel Baia, whose long popular terrace occupies a broad forecourt above the beach; its rooms overlook the bay itself. In case you need more information, you will find another Turismo.

Cascais is compact, and tea-rooms, a John Bull pub and announcements for bridge clubs betray an English influence. As you come out of the station, the main commercial area – around Praca Dr Francisco Sa Carneiro – is straight ahead, and the pleasant pedestrian shopping street Rua Frederico Arouca is off to your left. Head down the latter. A small street off to the left, as you walk down, is the **Rua das Flores** in which virtually every establishment is a restaurant. Among them, in a tight cluster, are Pimentão with bright red-and-green awning (Portugal's national colours), O Pipas, O Castro, O Pescador, O Batel. My own preference for a place to dine is out of town along the Guincho, but if you've been ensnared by the charms of Cascais pick from the Rua das Flores bouquet according to whichever ambience, menu and price pleases you.

You'll have the best view of Cascais on the **Avenida Dom Carlos** which rises above the bay and leads to the Cidadela, a military fort which is still in use but which has a display of weaponry outside. You are now in the Largo da Assuncão. On the right is a church, the **Igreja da Nossa Senhora de Assunção**, with a painted wooden ceiling, 18th-century *azulejos* and paintings by two of Portugal's finest artists, José Malhoa and, from an earlier period, Josefa de Obidos.

Opposite is **Ceramicarte**, stocking excellent local pottery. Just to the north is the **Museu do Mar**, museum of the sea, which captures much of the seafaring tradition of this town. Heading down the other wall of the Cidadela you'll pass another exhibition space and then the striking **Castro Guimaraes Palace** and **library** which now houses the **Municipal Museum**, strong on art and archaeology.

Continue along this road, passing a selection of hotels, and you come on to the **Estrada da Boca do Inferno** (the mouth of hell), a row of caverns in the cliffs in which spray can rise in fierce fountains. To the right is a row of stalls selling crafts, clothing and colourful junk. Keep going along this road and you'll see on your right brash new buildings which have been constructed in an area beside the large, exclusive **Quinta da Marinha**, an estate long regarded as the domain of the very rich. It boasts a golf club, stables, and occasionally holds horse-racing competitions.

From here stretch magnificent cliffs interspersed with fine beaches. If you have a car you can quickly reach **Hotel do Guincho**, once a fort, or the popular **Estalagem Muchaxo** whose pool is set above the long beach. The road leads, in another 13km (8 miles) or so, to the **Cabo da Roca**, continental Europe's most westerly point.

Even if you've skipped that drive, or not bothered to hire a car, you can still enjoy a fine dinner beside the sea on the terrace of **Restaurante Furnas** (tel: 486 92 43). It's about 1km (½ mile) from the Boca do Inferno on the Guincho road down a dirt turnoff. The seafood is excellent, though not cheap. A dish of prawns, olives and fresh goat cheese arrives at your table before you even order.

Take a taxi back to Cascais and the train into Lisbon. With a car, return via the Marginal with the Tejo on your right all the way. If you crave more excitement, try your luck at the Casino in Estoril or disco the night away at **Coconuts**, near the lighthouse off the Estrada da Boca do Inferno in Cascais.

7. Mafra's Monastery-Palace

A country drive to see a masterpiece of 18th-century architecture.

A king yearned for an heir, and made a vow. A child was born and a monastery built. Now come the adjectives: massive, monumental, gigantic, vast: words that fail to describe the scale of the huge **monastery-palace** at Mafra built between 1717 and 1735 to celebrate the birth of a daughter to King João V and his Austrian queen. To see this colossal palace (Wednesday–Monday 10am–1pm and 2–5pm, closed Tuesday and holidays; admission charge in-

The library at Mafra

The Monastery-palace

cludes a guided tour) you'll need a car – though it's a popular excursion for coach tours.

The small town of **Mafra** with its celebrated landmark is a little over 40km (25 miles) northwest of Lisbon. With a good map, you can reach it by taking minor roads west and north of Lisbon which will provide an agreeable impression of the capital's surprisingly rural outskirts. Alternatively you could take the brand new A8 stretch of expressway which has been cut into the IC1 motorway as far as Malveira, just east of Mafra. I suggest you go out the slow way, and return by the fast route. For refreshment or a meal you'll see small cafés and restaurants across the street from the Mafra monastery.

The guided tour of the monastery-palace lasts some 45 minutes and takes you from the apartments of King João V at one end of the enormous structure, through the splendid baroque library, great domed basilica and plainer quarters (such as the pharmacy and many long galleries and corridors) to the queen's apartments at the other end some 250m (820ft) away. It's a domestic arrangement that, in the context, seems surprising.

The architect of Mafra was the German-born Johann Ludwig. After training in Italy and working in Portugal for the Jesuits, he became known as João Ludovice. (Not all his work is as daunting: he also designed, as a palace, the pleasant Solar do Vinho do Porto you may have visited on *Day 2*.) It

Zé Franco the potter

seemed incredible, at the time, that Mafra would ever be completed. Armies of workmen were brought in; at one point there were 45,000 stonemasons and labourers. Artists came from abroad, including a French sculptor, Claude de Laprade from Avignon, the Italian Alessandro Giusti and an Irishman, Eugene Egen, to work on the organs. The bells came from Brussels; a single carillon of 50 bells cost a shipload in gold. 'So cheap?' the king is said to have exclaimed. 'I'll take two.' (You may, if you're lucky, hear a *carilhonista* practising; carillon concerts are held from time to time.)

Guides may spout some of the statistics of the great building:

5,200 doorways, 2,500 windows, the armies of workers, the numbers that died. In 1720 the French ambassador reported to his king that Mafra was a monumental failure and all the money in Iberia was insufficient to pay for it. Yet in 1730 the basilica was consecrated and in 1735 the palace was complete.

There is a marvellous book, if you can find it, based on historical events around the building of Mafra. A classic of modern literature by José Saramago, it's called *Memorial do Convento* (in English *Baltasar and Blimunda*). You'll read of the horror of the Inquisition, the story of the machine that flew, of Domenico Scarlatti's stint as music teacher to the king's children and of the enduring love between the leading characters.

If you have time for a short detour, carry on 4km (2½ miles) to Sobreiro in the Torres Vedras direction (you'll pass the Mafra tourist office). Leaving several *olarias* (potteries), to your right as you go, stop at the group of painted cottages with blue window frames and a miniature windmill. A popular **pottery shop** here, it is also the workshop of the elderly and eminent potter Zé (or José) Franco. He himself won't sell you his pieces (mainly religious figures or jovial Bacchus) personally, but the shop will. The price for a 30cm (1ft) high figure is upwards of 20,000$00; for the larger ones, expect to pay 40,000$00 or more.

8. Ferryboat across the Tejo

Cross the river for a seafood meal then take a bus up to the Cristo-Rei sanctuary.

You can see Lisbon's sights from the river in an afternoon cruise offered between April and October by the Transtejo company. It starts from the ferry stage at the Praça do Comércio.

But all year round you can cross the Tejo by ferryboat. This way, instead of tourists for company, you have commuters from the *Outra Banda*, as *lisboetas* call the Tejo's southern bank. Another bonus is that a short bus ride from the terminal takes you to the feet of Christ – the tall, solitary **Cristo-Rei** that stands arms outstretched near the Tejo bridge. Echoing the more famous Christ of Rio de Janeiro, the statue, the work of Francisco Franco, dates to 1959, in the Salazar era. Pressure is currently being taken off the ferries (and

The Tejo bridge with Cristo-Rei behind

Typical Tejo ferry

the dramatic Ponte 25 de Abril downstream) by a new bridge which should be visible upstream at the Expo 98 site.

For your crossing, be sure to catch an orange boat (called *cacilheiros* by commuters, after the port of Cacilhas on the other side). Blue boats go elsewhere. Arriving at the Outra Banda, the aroma of charcoal and grilled fish is strong as you step ashore. You will also realise that Cacilhas has missed out on some of the infrastructure cash available across the water, but it is nonetheless characterful for all that. This is a popular weekend and evening destination for *lisboetas*, for the seafood restaurants are many, informal, and excellent. *Caldeirada a fragateira*, a tasty fish stew, is a speciality. Go round the corner into the main street beyond the bus terminal and look at some of the window displays.

For the **Santuário Nacional de Cristo-Rei** (Monday to Friday 9am–6.45pm, weekends 9am–7.15pm), you need to take the No 10 bus from the right island in the ferryside bus terminal. There's a bus every 25 minutes or so. It's a 75$00 ride of about 10 or 15 minutes through the less than thrilling town of Almada and up to the sanctuary. You'll see first an **Edifício do Acolhimento**, a Catholic welcome centre whose design – and presence – is somewhat controversial. A few steps beyond here, Cristo-Rei (Christ the King) stands high and mighty – 110m (360ft), of which 82m (269ft) are pedestal and 28m (91ft) the robed figure.

There is a small fee to take the elevator to the platform at the top of the pedestal. Even without that,

Cristo-Rei

the view across the bridge, below you and humming with traffic, is spectacular. There's a cafeteria at the base of the monument if you want a coffee, and ample space for a car if you have driven here. (From Lisbon, come across the bridge and take the signs for Almada and Cristo-Rei.)

If you have come by ferryboat, be sure to avoid returning during the rush hours, 5–7.30pm; otherwise you will be just one more crushed commuter.

Lisbon's Aqueduto das Aguas Livres

9. A Walk along the Great Aqueduct

Several times a year the Great Aqueduct is open to groups of people who want to walk it – or at least a section of it. To find out when, you should fax or telephone the Museu de Água (tel: 813 55 22; fax: 813 99 74). EPAL, the water authority, will organise excursions on demand.

The vast **Aqueduto das Aguas Livres** (Aqueduct of Free Waters), astonished all Lisbon (which badly needed the water) and every visitor to Lisbon when it was constructed between 1732 and 1748, and completed in 1835. William Beckford, a wealthy Englishman and witty diarist who stayed for long periods in Portugal from 1787, was deeply impressed by it. Well he might have been, for its 109 arches across 18½km (11½ miles) resisted with barely a quiver the Great Earthquake of 1755 that destroyed most of Lisbon. The main engineer involved in the project was Manuel da Maia, with Custódio Vieira as architect. Understandably, the Marquês de Pombal was quick to call on the services of both men in the rebuilding of the capital following the quake.

Access to the aqueduct, still partly in operation and cared for by the EPAL water company, is in **Campolide**. A narrow door leads straight on to the aqueduct: it is broad enough for visitors to walk in pairs and the walls are high enough to prevent vertigo. The walk takes half-an-hour. It emerges at **Monsanto** in north Lisbon, the forested outskirts. It's safe as houses, they'll tell you. Bring the kids (some do). The guides may tell you about a famous murderer who lured his victims to the aqueduct and then tossed them over the wall.

Even if you don't feel inspired to walk the length of the aqueduct, look out for it on your left as you take the train to Sintra (*see itinerary 10, pages 60–3*)

EXCUR

10. Sintra, Byron's 'glorious Eden'

The summer resort of kings. If you want to lunch in style at Hotel Palácio (see text) book ahead (Tel: 923 32 00).

A small town 28km (17 miles) northeast of Lisbon on a cool and fertile highland, **Sintra** was the summer resort of Portuguese royalty for centuries. Lavishly praised by generations of travellers for the beauty of its forest glades and craggy mountains, enchanting views and eccentric buildings – some harmonious, others follies of caprice and great wealth – Sintra is still irresistible today. You don't need a car to get there. Frequent trains make the inexpensive 45-minute journey from Lisbon's Rossio station.

From Sintra station, turn left out of the station building and walk downhill. The old town will appear on the hill ahead. On the

Sintra's Royal Palace

way you pass the cheerful town hall with its Hansel-and-Gretel steeple and, announced by a mouthwatering aroma, a small bakery which makes delicious sweet cheese tarts, the classic *queijadas* Sintra folk have been devouring for at least 800 years. You can buy packets of six to take away or eat them on the spot; there's a charming tea-room. (If you come by car from Lisbon, head west as if to Estoril but go slowly and stay in the right hand lane to catch the Sintra turnoff.)

Right in the centre of Sintra's *vila-velha* (old town), distinguished by its prominent twin conical chimneys stands the Palácio Nacional, the

SIONS

Royal Palace (10am–1pm; 2–5pm, closed Wednesday and holidays). Most of what you see today was rebuilt over a Moorish palace in the 14th century by King João I. King Manuel I (1495–1521) added a wing and a tower. The tiles in the Arab Room are particularly striking. Be sure to look up at the ceilings: one is painted with 27 swans, another – a permanent reprimand to gossiping court ladies – with magpies.

A face of Regaleira

Up the street a little way beyond the palace you will find a **Turismo** office, which can supply a map of Sintra and information on local events (Sintra has a first-rate annual music festival). If you walk straight on up and round the bend, you will come to the gate, on your right, of the long-closed **Estalagem dos Cavaleiros**. Peer through to see the small plaque stating that this was where Lord Byron stayed during his sojourn in Sintra. On your left over the next stretch is a section of **Regaleira**, one of Sintra's oddest and grandest *quintas* (estates) ending with the florid mansion itself.

Opening on the right in about 250m (820ft) is the lawn of the **Hotel Palácio de Seteais**, built in the 18th century as a stylish residence by Daniel Gildemeester, a Dutch consul and diamond merchant. From the lawn, look up to the hills and you'll see, if it isn't misty, the outline of the Moors' castle to the left and, on a higher crag (some 470m/ 1,542ft) to the right, the Gothic turrets and golden domes of Pena palace, painted a startling terracotta and yellow.

The Palácio hotel does an

Dining in the Hotel Palácio

Entering Pena palace

excellent formal lunch for 5,900$00 in their splendid painted dining-room. As a guest, you are welcome to wander through the gardens, enjoy the panoramic view through the arch and lean against the very boulder that inspired Byron to pen his romantic verses. If you prefer to lunch in Sintra, you'll find several restaurants tucked into its narrow streets.

From Seteais it's another 2½km (1½ miles) along a bosky road, lined by *quintas*, to **Monserrate**, an exotic, pseudo-oriental 1860s gem in magnificent gardens which was originally the property of a rich Englishman. The house is closed, but the gardens are open. It's easy to get to with a car, but too far without one.

Meanwhile back in Sintra, drive up or take a cab to **Pena palace** (same hours as Sintra's royal palace but closed Monday and holidays). Cab drivers will take you there, and back, for about 3,000$00. You could also walk. Climbing up the steep Estrada da Pena from Sintra, there's a walkers' entrance at 2½km (1½miles) to the **Castelo dos Mouros**, Moorish castle (10am–5pm), and a wonderful view down to Sintra. Higher up is a walkers' side entrance to the Pena gardens. The main gate, and parking, is 300m (980ft) further on.

Pena palace is the 1840s concoction of Ferdinand, the Saxe-Coburg consort of Portugal's Queen Maria da Glória. The gardens and ferns are impressive, the wild mix of styles in the palace gloriously bizarre. Its low-ceilinged, intimate rooms are exotic, with strong Arabic influences. If you have a car, leave by the road you came up and bear left for 5km (3 miles) to the small **Convento dos Capuchos** (Capuchos monastery) cut into Sintra rock in 1560. Lined with cork, covered with moss, it was, remarked King Philip II of Spain when he was also ruler of Portugal, the poorest convent in his kingdom. Among other distinctive buildings in Sintra that are walkable from the town centre is the library and museum in the former Palácio de Valenças.

Where Byron stayed

Sintra can be crowded, especially in summer. It's also lively on the second and fourth Sunday of the month when the neighbouring parish of São Pedro holds a well-attended fair. If you go, you'll see a fine selection of handicrafts, mainly pottery, and antiques. Beware fakes! Restaurants tend to fill up quickly, but you will find cheeses, *chouriços* (smoked sausage) and bread at the market. Have a *fartura*, a doughnut quick-fried on the spot and dipped in sugar and cinnamon.

11. South to Sesimbra, Setúbal and more

Sesimbra's fishing harbour, the wildly beautiful Serra da Arrábida, Bacalhôa's classical garden and tiles, Azeitão cheese (for a picnic?), wine cellars, the castle-pousadas at Setúbal and Palmela. An excursion for those with a car.

Start by crossing the Tejo by the Ponte 25 de Abril, 25th April bridge (Sul Ponte, signs say) to the southbound motorway A2/IP1. Turn off at the Sesimbra sign after about 10km (6 miles). The road (378) goes due south for 22km (13½ miles) to **Sesimbra**, a bustling fishing port with a crenellated castle for backdrop. It's nearly always lively. In these waters swordfish are the prime catch. Grab a coffee at a café, if you need one, and tear yourself away. Once you're out of town, take the right-hand turning (379) toward **Setúbal**. In 11km (7 miles) you come to **Vila Nogueira de Azeitão**. A fine cheese is made here, one of the best in Portugal. Market day is the first Sunday in the month but you could buy an Azeitão cheese for a picnic in the Serra (if you don't want to lunch formally) at the café at the São Lourenço corner. They're not cheap: 1,260$00 for a small round cheese.

The Serra da Arrábida

At this corner you'll see the Arrábida sign, but carry on for another 5km (3 miles) to **Vila Fresca de Azeitão** and the wine cellars of the eminent winemakers **José Maria da Fonseca**. Visitors are welcome at the 'casa de Lancers' from 9–11.30am and 2–5pm, except Sunday and holidays. Opposite the big Rodoviaria Nacional bus station and almost hidden by trees is the entrance to the **Quinta de Bacalhôa**, dating from the 15th century. Privately owned, it's

In the Serra

a national monument where you may visit the gardens (1–5pm; closed Sunday). The property once belonged to the son of Portugal's first viceroy to India who built the towered garden pavilion with its tile panel of *Susanna and the Elders*, the oldest (1565) in Portugal.

Go back to the São Lourenço corner to take the country road to the Serra – mountains – and **Parque Natural da Arrábida**. The road is winding and narrow, but it's an attractive approach to the wonderfully rugged natural park where, protected by Cape Espichel, land and sea meet in striking counterpoint. From the depths of the sea the Serra rises a sheer 500m (1,640ft). Science describes this rolling heathland as a glacial relict, its primitive forests preserved when glaciers melted. The 12km (7½ miles) across the Serra is powerfully dramatic; wild slopes contrast with the intense blue of the sea below. Come in Spring and the park is bright with flowers. The old monastery snug in the hills has been resurrected as part of Lisbon University. The cement factory, huge and hideous, that mars your descent should be ignored.

On the outskirts of Setúbal, you could turn sharp right to drive along the park's lower road where there is access to several pleasant beaches, **Portinho da Arrábida** being one of them. However, avoid this coast road on Sunday in summer, when all Setúbal heads for the beach and it's jammed with traffic.

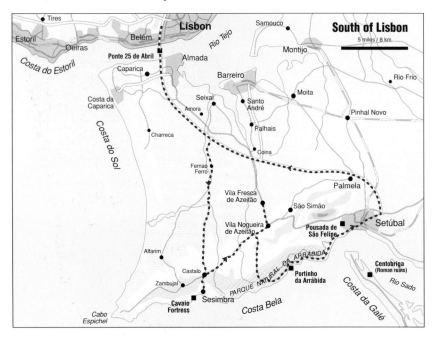

On the beach

Setúbal is a fishing port and industrial town. Its loveliest building by far is the **Igreja de Jesus**, its spiralling columns and rope-like ribs Manueline (late Gothic) art at its most glorious. You'll find the church in the Avenida de Luisa Todi; the adjoining cloister is now a museum. Carry on up the Avenida for 500m (1,640ft) and, with a forbidding fortress outline looming high ahead, turn right into the narrow Rua Marquês da Corta and follow signs up the twisting road to the **Pousada de São Felipe**. Built at the end of the 16th century to the order of King Philip II of Spain, it's one of Portugal's most stoutly fortified castle-*pousadas* – you even enter on foot through a discouraging tunnel. The view from the terrace across the broad Sado river estuary is overwhelming. If you haven't picnicked in the hills or stopped on a beach on the way you could, perhaps, have lunch here. The dining-room, though modest in size, has the sea beside it and fresh fish on the menu.

At Setúbal, you're only 12km (7 miles) from another impressive castle-*pousada* in **Palmela**. Sink into a large comfy chair in what were once cloisters and remind yourself that King Afonso Henriques snatched this great fortification from the Moors in the 12th century. A church and monastery of the São Tiago (St James) Order came later. Buried in the church is a bastard son of King João II. When his father died, it was a cousin who gained the throne, vast wealth, and the nickname of Manuel the Fortunate. The dining-room, once a refectory, is long and elegant; first-class meals are served with style.

Tea in the cloisters? A drink in the bar? Dinner in the *pousada*'s handsome dining-room? This is the place to linger a while. Here, via the motorway, you're only about 25 km (15 miles) from Lisbon and can get back to the city easily and quickly.

Columns in the Igreja de Jesus

Shopping

The Baixa and the Chiado

The itinerary proposed for Day 2 (*see page 27*) takes you through Lisbon's main shopping areas, the **Baixa** and the **Chiado**. It mentions the shoe shops in Rua 1 de Dezembro close to the Rossio. Portugal's leather shoes, though more expensive lately, remain good value, especially for visitors from Northern Europe. There is a wide variety of shops in the Baixa's Rua Augusta where, for embroidered linen, you'll find Madeira House at No 135. Numerous shops sell regional handicrafts and souvenirs. Up from the Baixa,

Books for sale

at 61B Rua Castilho, is the **Centro de Turismo e Artesanato** (daily 9am–8pm). It will pack and ship for you.

Lisbon is no centre of high fashion but quality clothes are there

Fábrica Viúva Lamego

– I've listed some shops in Rua Garrett (the Chiado). Walk up Rua Garrett via Rua do Carmo. At No 87 is **Ana Salazar**, a leading designer.

Silver and gold, too, are good in Lisbon. The gold is always 19¼ carats. Filigree jewellery is a Portuguese craft. One of the loveliest shops is **Ouriversaria Aliança** at 50 Rua Garrett.

Up the street, at 18 Largo do Chiado is **Vista Alegre** for Portugal's quality porcelain. Nearby, at 91 Rua do Alecrim, you'll find classical ceramics and *azulejos* at Sant'Anna. And don't forget the tile-fronted **Fábrica Cerâmica Viúva Lamego** in the otherwise tawdry Largo do Intendente (see my AM itinerary 5 on Lisbon's architecture). Rua Augusta Rosa up by the cathedral has several shops with antiques and remarkable curiosities, often religious.

Bairro Alto

You'll find more antiques in the area of the **Bairro Alto**, on the long street that is a continuation of the Rua do Alecrim. At 70 Rua Dom Pedro V, **Solar** specialises in antique *azulejos*; at No 111 **Xairel** tends toward regional pieces. Remember, too, that cork is one of Portugal's major products. You'll see cork table mats and cork carvings in craft shops. The **Casa das Cortiças-Mr Cork**, at 4 Rua da Escola Politécnica, is devoted to cork. On a related matter, **port wine** is purely Portuguese; the **Solar do Vinho do Porto** is handy at 45 Rua São Pedro de Alcântara.

Amoreiras Shopping Centre

For younger *lisboetas*, this is the place to shop. It's bright, cheerful and self-contained. The shopping centre, on two floors in a five-towered apartment and office complex, has banks, a post office, 10 cinemas, a supermarket, a chapel, art galleries, a variety of eating places and some 300 shops from furniture and linen, to music, books, china and chocolate. Clothing boutiques dot the 'streets' of the shopping centre. Quality porcelain and glass producers are here too: **Vista Alegre** at No 2080 and **Atlantis** at the foot of the steps in Praça dos Cedros. An information desk is there to help you find what you want.

Cascaishopping

Out near Cascais, beside the new motorway, Cascaishopping is the latest shopping complex (just as popular as Amoreiras). Big names like Benetton draw the crowds though prices tend to be higher. For easy shopping closer to town, you might like the **Centro Comercial de Alvalade** and the fashionable but generally expensive **Avenida da Roma**.

Markets

For crafts – baskets and pottery in particular – cheap clothes, boots and shoes, linens and household goods, rustic cheeses and sausages, and all the fun of the fair head for the **Feira da Ladra** (Thieves' Fair), **Campo de Santa Clara**, on Tuesday and Saturday, **Cascais** on Wednesday, **Carcavelos** on Thursdays, and São Pedro in **Sintra** on the second and fourth Sunday of each month.

Market Produce

Eating Out

Lisbon's metropolitan population of 600,000 delights in wine and food and the city consequently has a large number of restaurants, some fine and fancy, many cheap and simple. Social life is further enlivened by popular tea-houses such as **Ferrari** (2 Escadinhas de São Francisco, off Rua Ivens) and numerous *tascas*, simple bars or tiny restaurants, particularly plentiful in the Bairro Alto. But what are people eating?

Tempting table

Perennial favourites are stews, in particular *feijoada* (pork and beans), the Alentejano dish, *pézinhos de co-entrada* (pig's trotters with coriander), eels from Aveiro and river trout from the Minho. A fish stew is a *caldeirada*. *Caldo verde*, a kale-and-potato soup, is served from the classiest restaurant to the meanest *tasca*.

Portuguese food is rustic, savoury, stacked with herbs but rarely peppery or heavily spiced. If dishes look huge, ask for *uma meia dose*, a half-portion. Unfortunately restaurants often spoil their own marvellous meals by serving on cold plates.

You'll find *bacalhau* (dried cod) on many menus; dubbed *o fiel amigo*, the faithful friend, it's a national passion. Allegedly, there are 365 recipes for *bacalhau*, one for each day of the year. *Bacalhau à Bras* is dried cod flaked with olives, potatoes and onions into scrambled eggs. It also comes as *pasteis*, rissoles. By the way, with *bacalhau*, you drink red not white wine. Many restaurants serve fresh fish like sole and bream, and shellfish ranging from the modest clam to the pricey lobster.

As for Portuguese sweets, many eggs and too much sugar go into assorted pastries and cakes. A particularly delicious *soufflé* is *pudim Molotov*. You may also come across so-called 'convent sweets', made by nuns. In the 18th century nuns raised money by selling their

Bacalhau is a national passion

sweets and small cakes, and some still do. One you're likely to encounter in restaurants is a divine confection called *Toucinho do Ceu,* food from heaven (made from sugar, almonds and many egg yolks). Coffee (*café*) is medium-strong; a small, strong espresso is a *bica*; weak black is a *carioca.* All restaurants must offer a tourist menu, a full meal at an inclusive price. A house wine is also obligatory, and included in the price of a tourist menu, though it may be only a glass. Many restaurants are closed on Sunday. Usual eating hours are 12.30–2.30pm and 8–10pm. All establishments have a complaints book, *Livro de reclamações.* You're unlikely to need it.

In the listings that follow, 'Expensive' = over 15,000$00 for two; 'Moderate' = 6,000–15,000$00; 'Inexpensive' = under 6,000$00.

TAGIDE
18 Largo Academia das Belas Artes
Tel: 342 0720
A top-ranking restaurant whose decor – cool blue and white tile panels – is as pleasant as its food. A verandah offers views. International as well as Portuguese menu. Expensive.

BRASUCA
7 Rua João Rosa
Tel: 342 85 42
Brazilian restaurant popular with journalists and academics. Moderate.

BOTA ALTA
35-37 Travessa Queimada
Tel: 342 79 59
Very popular with the intelligentsia. Excellent Portuguese food in a cheerful, crowded atmosphere. Inexpensive.

CASA DA COMIDA
1 Travessa das Amoreiras
Tel: 388 53 76
Smart and sophisticated, with a courtyard garden. The food ranges from traditional Portuguese dishes to frogs' legs. It's a 10-minute taxi ride from the centre of town, near Alcântara. Check the driver knows where it is. Expensive.

GAMBRINUS
23 Rua das Portas de Santo Antão
Tel: 342 14 66
In the centre of town, Gambrinus is much favoured by the city's notable families and well-off businessmen. Good fish and shellfish. Expensive.

CASA DO LEAO
Castelo San Jorge
Tel: 887 59 62
Pousada-run establishment within castle walls. Portuguese specialities.

PILE OU FACE
70 Rua Barroca
Tel: 342 23 45
Smart but relaxing French restaurant which takes food seriously. Moderate.

Staff at Sol Dourado

Seafood special

off the Praça dos Restauradores with fresh, tasty and cheap seafood. Popular with Portuguese families and foreigners. Quick friendly service. Inexpensive.

MALMEQUER BEMMEQUER
Largo de São Miguel
Tel: 887 65 35
Charming restaurant situated in Alfama. Inexpensive.

ARRAIAL
Rua Conde de Sabugosa, 113A,
1700 Lisbon
Tel: 849 73 43
Behind the Centro Comercial Roma. Go by metro to Roma station. Tasty Portuguese dishes, as well as seafood. Moderate.

TAVARES RICO
37 Rua da Misericórdia
Tel: 342 11 12
Lisbon's oldest restaurant. Sumptuous setting and a broad and enticing menu. First class cooking. Expensive.

CASANOSTRA
60 Travessa Poço da Cidade
Tel: 342 59 31
Italian dishes in a small low-cost Bairro Alto restaurant. Cool decor, art on the walls. Inexpensive.

SOL DOURADO
19–25 Rua Jardim do Regador
Tel: 347 25 70
A bright, unpretentious restaurant just

CONVENTUAL
45 Praça das Flores
Tel: 60 91 06
Pink decor with antiques. Good food and service. Offers at least one or two classical convent sweets. Expensive.

Fruit for dessert

In addition to the above, every neighbourhood has one or more modest restaurants with a standard menu, low prices, and television babbling from the wall. You won't go hungry. But, by way of contrast, don't forget the hotels. Five-star luxury costs less in Lisbon than in many other cities. The **Ritz** (tel: 383 20 20), above the Praça Marquês de Pombal, and the **Tivoli** (tel: 353 01 81), on the Avenida da Liberdade have restaurants that are highly esteemed (and expensive) for first-class cuisine. The **Tivoli Jardim** (tel: 353 99 71), tucked a little way behind its grander sister, has a pleasant ground-floor restaurant at modest prices.

Local Prawns

Nightlife

Lisbon's nightlife is as diverse as you would expect of a culture-conscious city. You'll find smooth bars and murky *tabernas*, music that's coolly classical, hot jazz or thunderous rock. There are local and city centre theatres – check a daily paper (*Público* or *Diário de Notícias*) to see what's on.

Little or no knowledge of Portuguese might hamper your enjoyment of drama but there's always a good spectacle, perhaps at the **Dona Maria II** theatre or the Estoril **Casino** (see below). Alternatively you could go to a bullfight at **Campo Pequeno** (starts at 10pm every Thursday and sometimes Saturday too). It is not as bloody as in Spain. For one thing there's no initial stabbing by a *picador*, though the bull is darted with *farpas*. For another, in Portugal they don't publicly kill the bull, but herd him out among steers. Stars of the show are *cavaleiros*, brilliantly skilled horsemen in satin embroidered coats. *Forcados*, local teams of eight young men who face the bull bare-handed are the *corrida's* unpaid heroes. Tickets at various prices can be bought at the arena or in advance

When the moon rises, Lisbon does not go to sleep

from the Restauradores kiosk. Cascais sometimes stages afternoon bullfights at the *praça de touros* (check upcoming programme with Cascais Turismo; tel: 486 82 04).

If you want something less brutal, try a performance of dressage by the **Escola Portuguesa da Arte Equestre** (performances are held on the last Wednesday of each month). The finest dressage horsemen in Portugal ride superb Lusitanos from the Alter Real (formerly royal) stables. Events are irregular, so check with Turismo in Restauradores for upcoming schedules. Performances are held either in Queluz Palace or the hippodrome at Campo Grande.

Opera and ballet are performed in brief seasons at the elegantly-tiered **São Carlos** theatre, but tickets are scarce. Concerts and ballet performances are held regularly at the **Gulbenkian Foundation**, which funds a symphony orchestra, ballet company, choral group and cultural events that include a lively programme of international modern dance. The Centro Cultural de Belém has a raft of events, details of which are published in its own monthly booklet, free from tourist offices and hotels.

Classical **music festivals** are held annually in Lisbon, Estoril and Sintra. Lisbon and Estoril both sponsor **jazz festivals**. You'll find jazz nightly at the **Hot Clube**, 38–39 Praça da Alegria (free weekdays; about 1,000$00 weekends). Top Portuguese rock groups like the Xutos e Pontapés and popular musicians headed by versatile rock guitarist Rui Veloso also appear in public performances. Don't miss

Dressage at Escola Portuguesa da Arte Equestre

the opportunity, if it arises, to go to any performance by the eminent guitarist Carlos Paredes. The national, passionately emotional music of *fado* can be heard any night in the **Bairro Alto**. For dinner and *fado* (at a price) go to **Arcadas do Faia** (54–56 Rua da Barroca; tel: 342 19 23), **A Severa** (51–61 Rua das Gaveas; tel: 346 12 04) or **Alfaia** (24 Travessa da Queimada; tel: 346 12 32). Wander into the small bars and *tascas* in and around Rua Diário de Notícias late at night and you will probably be able to hear amateur *fado – fado vadio –* for the price of a cheap drink. Two mellow guitars and the sound of *saudade* – hopeless yearning – comprise an essential part of the Portuguese soul.

The Bairro Alto has the busiest and most varied nightlife. People who can't stand *fado* go there to drink in a wide range of bars, some casual, others catering to a better-dressed clientele who ring doorbells to enter. One of these is the **Pavilhão Chinês** (9pm–2am) at 89–92 Rua Dom Pedro V. It is calm, carpeted and upholstered

Fado in full flow

and, even in a chandelier-lit pool room, crammed with assorted antiques, the personal collection of the owner. Another sophisticated bar with an arty, international ambience is the **Nova** (10pm–2am) at 261 Rua da Rosa.

For cocktails like TGV (tequila, gin, vodka) or the fiery Flaming Shot, go to the inexpensive **Termas da Atalaia** (10pm–2am) at 108 Rua da Atalaia. Around the corner, (105–7 Rua da Barroca) the **Cena de Copos** (10pm–2am) offers a potent B-52 (Bailey's, Tia Maria and Absinthe, set alight and served with straw).

When the bars close, the Bairro Alto is still humming. Clubs and discos abound, some of them very, very selective. If you make it into the **Fragil** disco (11pm–4am), 126 Rua da Atalaia, you will find yourself among Lisbon's trendiest. Another option is **Incognito** (11pm–3.30am), 85 Rua dos Poiais de São Bento, with good music and a mixed crowd.

The other area for fast night action is Santos, off the Avenida 24 de Julho. The **Plateau** (11 Rua das Escadinhas da Praia) is the watering hole of top people prepared to pay top prices (minimum 5,000$00). Just down the street, at No 1, is the more accessible (1,000$00) **Kremlin** (10.30pm–4am; weekends reopens 6–8am), the liveliest nightspot in Lisbon. The largest disco in Lisbon is the **Alcântara-mar** (11pm–4am), 5–11 Rua da Cozinha Económica. The admission fee includes one drink.

Out at Estoril and Cascais, there's plenty of nightlife, including the **Casino** (3pm–3am). Go for dinner (8.30pm), the show (star entertainer and dances), the tables and the slot machines. There are two rules governing entry: you must take a passport and gamblers must be over 18 years old. Prices range from 6,000$00 – 9,000$00 on average, more on nights when international stars perform. You can play all the classical games – roulette, blackjack, etc – and the slots. The top jackpot is one of the biggest in Europe.

For an evening drink (open until midnight), you'll find the **Tamariz** opposite the Estoril train station. As to discos, it's relatively calm at the **Louvre**, on the Marginal about 1km (½ mile) before Estoril. For rock music at full blast, head for the **2000**, right under the Formula 1 Autodromo track (stays open until 4am). The trendiest disco of all, and not expensive, is **Coconuts** (11pm–6am), off the Estrada da Boca do Inferno. You can dance until you drop – and cool off in their swimming pool.

Calendar of Special Events

When recently the Portuguese government proposed to amend the holiday calendar there was an outcry. Plans to transfer holidays to the nearest Monday, to replace the All Saints' Day holiday (1 November) with All Souls' Day (2 November) and to abolish two bank holidays, Shrove Tuesday and Corpus Christi, were met with protest from the Church, workers' unions and the municipalities. 'We won't allow the celebration of the Day of Santo António (13 June) to be turned into a triviality,' said the mayor. Santo António is celebrated only in Lisbon, and it is very special to *Lisboetas*. Needless to say, the proposed changes were abandoned.

Santo António procession

JANUARY–APRIL

New Year apart, Lisbon's calendar of special events kicks off with the weekend revelry of **Carnival**, a moveable feast that precedes Lent. On the second Sunday of Lent, the neighbourhood of Graça holds the annual procession of the Brotherhood of Santa Cruz dos Passos, founded in 1634. Good Friday means Church for some, a day off work for others. On the anniversary of the 1974 revolution, 25 April, there's usually a parade.

MAY–AUGUST

1 May is **Labour Day**, and **10 June** a day jointly honouring Portugal and its epic national poet, Camões, but June is the best month to be in Lisbon

74

from the point of view of festivals. Lisbon-born St Anthony of Padua is very special to *lisboetas*, with St John (São João) and St Peter (São Pedro), not far behind, and costly preparations are made in every neighbourhood for the *festas dos santos populares* (festivals of the popular saints) which last from the middle to the end of June. On the night of **Santo António** (12 June), the eve of his feast day on the 13th, the city pays homage to its favourite saint with *marchas* – a cheerfully noisy parade down the Avenida da Liberdade in which costumed groups and bands from every neighbourhood take part. After that, the place to be is **Alfama** where coloured lights sparkle in every decorated street and square, sardines are grilled by the thousand, wine flows, music plays, people dance – and buy or sell pots of basil for luck. Everyone is welcome. On the night of **São João**, 23 June before his holiday on the 24th, and the night of **São Pedro**, 28 June for the 29th, it's almost as festive. Then, with a last burst of fireworks, Lisbon's *bairros* take down the decorations for another year.

Outside Lisbon, Cascais celebrates its **Festa do Mar**, festival of the sea, between 12–29 June, coinciding with the popular saints' festivities in Lisbon. In Santarém, the Ribatejo town an hour's drive northeast of Lisbon, the week-long **Feira do Ribatejo**, an agricultural fair with a strong horsey flavour, begins on the first Friday in June; horse-riding *campinos*, the Ri-

batejo herdsmen, wear their colourful red-and-green traditional costume.

SEPTEMBER-DECEMBER

Also in Santarém, a **Festival Nacional de Gastronomia** is held in late October, providing opportunities to taste regional cooking at its best. In November, at Golegã, near Santarém, is the annual **Feira Nacional do Cavalo**, the national horse fair, when Portugal's finest Lusitanos are on display.

The big day in November, however, is **Dia de São Martinho** (St Martin's Day), on the 11th, when the year's new wine is tasted – if pleasing, again and again – as well as potent *aguapé*, which is made from grape pulp with chestnuts. On 1 December, **Restoration Day**, the Duke of Bragança, heir to a non-existent throne, addresses a monarchist gathering. As Christmas approaches Lisbon's city centre is a blaze of prettily patterned street lights.

Alfama celebrates Santo António

PRACTICAL information

By Air

TAP Air Portugal is Portugal's national airline and it has wide international links. Moreover many major airlines make non-stop direct flights to Lisbon from capital cities in Europe and other continents. Links with London are particularly good. From New York, too, there are several flights a week.

Lisbon International Airport is on the outskirts of the city. A taxi to the city centre costs about 1500$00. Every taxi has a meter but – watch out – is entitled to charge an excess if your luggage exceeds 30kg (66lb). If the driver doesn't charge this item, you could pay him a 10 percent tip. The Aero Bus (No 91) travels direct between the airport, the main ho-

Road and rail routes

tels, the Rossio and Cais do Sodre station, in the city centre just off the Praça do Comércio.

By Rail

Lisbon is not yet linked to the superfast TVG system, but there's a busy international (and national) train service. Trains from across Europe arrive at Santa Apolónia station.

By Road

Good roads link Portugal with its neighbour Spain at numerous border points. Main east-west routes to Lisbon are from Seville via Beja; from Badajoz via Elvas; from Salamanca via Viseu. Driving from England, via the Channel ferries, allow three days; or, via Plymouth-Santander, two. Yes, there are drivers who boast of doing it faster. Don't try. Road accident figures are appallingly high.

TRAVEL ESSENTIALS

When to Visit

November to February in Lisbon is rainy and often grey but even winters are comparatively mild – average temperature in December and January is 12°C (53°F).

76

The National Assembly

The hottest month is August (22°C/72°F) when the city is also at its most crowded. June is fun, packed with events including the saint's day *festas*. But there is always something happening and, in practical terms, there's no time when it is inadvisable to come.

Visas and Passports

EC nationals, Australians, Americans and Canadians need nothing more than a valid passport for a three-month stay.

Customs

You're allowed to bring in as much currency as you like. Non-EC members can bring 400 cigarettes, one bottle of spirits, two of wine, 50g (1¾oz) of perfume; EC-members have guide levels of 800 cigarettes, 10 litres of spirit and 90 litres of wine. Customs keep a close watch for drugs, which are illegal.

Clothing

It's never freezing in Lisbon but, in winter, bring a coat, anorak, or mac to keep out chill winds and rain. In summer, bring a sweater for evenings and a light waterproof just in case. Lisbon's a city of hills and cobbled streets, so bring comfortable walking shoes. For classy dining, smarter establishments prefer men to wear jacket and tie but are accustomed to tasteful informality. In most places, casual gear will suffice. During summer or on days out of town, don't forget sunglasses and sunscreen lotion.

Electricity

Portugal's electricity is 220/240 volts AC, but plugs are two-pin for round holes. If you need to use appliances with a three-pin plug, bring an adaptor (some hotels have them).

Time Differences

Portugal's brief fling with European (EU) time is about to end (1996). Locals claim it made it too light in the evening and too dark on winter mornings. It now falls back into step with the UK.

GETTING ACQUAINTED

Geography

Portugal is situated in the southwest of Europe, with Spain to the north and east, the Atlantic Ocean south and west. It has an area of 88,684sq km, (34,216sq miles) and is nowhere more than 563km (350 miles) long or 225km (140 miles) wide. Lisbon's position on the north bank of the Tejo (Tagus) river, near its mouth on the lower part of the coast, is – to northerners – already the south. The Tejo river, which rises in Spain where it is called the Tajo, is 1,007km (626 miles) long and the longest river in Iberia.

Government and Economy

A democracy since the 25 April 1974 revolution, Portugal has been through a period of instability and a series of governments. In 1987 the Social Democrat party led by economist Aníbal Cavaco Silva won a majority vote in elections for the National Assembly and, repeated its victory in 1991. A socialist administration took over in 1995, led by António Guterres, with Dr Jorge Sampais succeeding Mário Soares as president.

Portugal has been a member of the EC (with Spain) since 1986. The benefits of structural funds and enthusiastic international investment have brought major improvements to infrastructure – most notably in roads and telephones. Steady liberalisation of the economy has been the pattern of recent years. Prices and salaries, which used to be low, are rising to meet the levels of richer European countries.

Bureaucracy, however, the heritage of Salazar's dictatorship, remains an irritating burden.

Religion

Portugal is Roman Catholic with a separation of powers between Church and State. The constitution establishes freedom of worship and in Lisbon there are numerous communities from other religions, among them Protestant, Muslim, Jewish and Jehovah's Witnesses. You will see many churches in Lisbon – and meet many people who never attend mass. Faith is strong in northern Portugal, weaker in the south. Lisbon, sophisticated in this as

After church

in much else, easily separates sacred from secular. In poorer neighbourhoods, religious beliefs are strong – and so is superstition.

How Not To Offend

The Portuguese – *lisboetas*, above all – are easygoing and tolerant. They are used to adjusting to foreign ways, whims and caprices. It's actually quite hard to offend them. A common-sense approach is best. For instance, men should not go shirtless into a church.

The Portuguese dote on small children – and expect you to, as well. They may be late for appointments; you should be on time. Everyone loves to talk, and no-one minds a good argument. If you *want* to offend, tell a Portuguese he or she is without honour.

You can trust nearly everybody, but not quite every taxi-driver. A few will take you for a ride in every sense (see *Taxis* below).

Population

An independent country since the 12th century, the 10.3 million Portuguese are proudly nationalistic. But history has contrived a distinguished meld of Celt, Moor, Jew and various invading visitors. Don't assume that blue eyes and fair hair are not Portuguese. A few Portuguese may be class-conscious, but the country is happily free of racism.

Money Matters

The *escudo* (it means shield) is the coin of national currency. New coins and notes are issued quite frequently and – annoyingly, if you've kept some from an earlier visit – are frequently withdrawn (a bank will usually change such notes). The *escudo* is written with a dollar sign, so that 150 *escudos* would be 150$00 – the two tiny noughts standing for *centavos*, of which there are theoretically 100 to an *escudo*. Hardly anyone bothers with them any more, paying or receiving. You may often hear the word *conto* which is 1,000$00, a thousand *escudos*.

There are many easy ways to change money in Lisbon. Traveller's cheques entail paying a commission, but the exchange rate is higher than for cash. Eurocheques are widely accepted, credit cards commonplace. There are also many cashpoints in city banks, especially in the Avenida da Liberdade. If you're driving out of town, you can quite often (but not always) use a Visa card to fill up, but garages add a 100$00 tax. There's no black market in currency.

Taxes

There's no airport tax but restaurants, hotels, shops are all obliged to add (or

Ready to change your money

include) IVA, value added tax. If you come from outside the EU you can benefit from Duty Free shopping (signs outside some shops promise duty-free prices). It's often worth checking elsewhere for duty-free prices, or a cash discount.

Tipping

Few Portuguese earn a decent income. Even though some restaurants include service in the bill, a tip of at least 10 percent is appreciated. Anyone who provides a service welcomes a tip. This includes helpful museum attendants and travel guides, hairdressers, hotel doormen and porters who carry your luggage. And, of course, all the good and decent taxi-drivers who charge you the right price.

GETTING AROUND

Taxis

Sterling service is provided cheaply (minimum 250$00) by the numerous black-and-green cabs of Lisbon. If you're in Lisbon for long, you will find you can't live without them. Probably the major fault among Lisbon taxi-drivers is that many drive too fast in heavily-populated areas. Some, honest and well-meaning, have an unfortunate habit, too, of taking off to look in the vaguest way for the address you want. (Write it down and/or carry a map.) The most experienced drivers make genuine detours to avoid traffic congestions. A meter operates within the city, but it is switched off at Lisbon's city limits.

All drivers carry lists of approved charges. Note, too, there is a radio-telephone service (different numbers for different areas; your hotel will know). You can – and should – hail cabs in the street, though it's not always easy to see if their lights are on or off, and there are a few places where they can't stop. Lunch times can be difficult: drivers want to go home to eat. In central Lisbon, a fast-moving cab rank is in the Rossio.

Train/Metro

Santa Apolónia is the main train station for national and international rail travel. The Rossio station serves such places as Queluz and Sintra. From Cais do Sodré, on the waterfront, electric trains make the run to and from Cascais. Lisbon also has a Metro system with 24 stations on lines that fan out in a rough W from the Rossio. Above ground, stations are marked with a big M. Tickets, for any distance, cost 70$00 if you buy them at the ticket counter, or 55$00 from a machine (which has instructions in English and French as well as Portuguese); you can also buy

Tour Lisbon by tram

booklets of tickets. Some station names may seem confusing: the Praça Marquês de Pombal station, for instance, is called Rotunda (the Praça's old name). Palhavã station will get you near the Gulbenkian Museum. There's also a Campo Pequeno station, close to the bullring. The zoo, if you want to go there, is at Sete Rios station. The newest stations, Laranjeiras among them, are marvellously decorated with *azulejos* by four of Portugal's top artists.

Bus/Tram

Lisbon can be packed with traffic, but the buses and trams go everywhere at surprising speed – except during rush hours (avoid them). You can get booklets of tickets (and maybe a route map but don't count on it) from the hatch at the back

Local transport

of the Santa Justa Elevador in the Baixa. The Lisboa Card (*see introduction to the itineraries, page 20*) allows free use of municipal transport and to most museums. Daily tours are offered to Lisbon and nearby sights by coaches parked below the park in Praça Marquês de Pombal. An antique tramcar makes daily 2-hour tours in summer from the Praça do Comércio.

Car

It's no pleasure driving in the city. For out-of-town trips there are numerous car hire companies at Lisbon airport and in the city. Avis, for example, has an office conveniently located in the garage of the Hotel Tivoli in the Avenida da Liberdade. Rental prices are cheaper than in most European countries. Petrol, however, costs more than in most countries. *Gasolina* is the word for petrol, *gasoleo* for diesel. Lead-free petrol (*sem chumbo*) is now widely available on main roads.

Ferry

To cross the Tejo, a crucial exercise for thousands of commuters living in south bank towns, there are ferries all day from the Praça do Comércio and from the Cais do Sodré. To cross downriver, there's a ferry at Belém which goes to the small port of Porto Brandão. Some people make the trip as an outing, often to eat lunch on the other side.

HOURS & HOLIDAYS

Business Hours

Most shops are open 9am–1pm and 3–7pm weekdays and mornings only on Saturdays. Offices often start later and stop earlier. Major banks are open Monday–Friday

8.30am–3pm. The bank at Lisbon airport is open 24 hours, as is the airport's post office. The most central post office in Lisbon, in the Restauradores, is open 8am–10pm.

Public Holidays

Fixed dates are: New Year's Day, **1 January**; Liberty Day, **25 April**; Labour Day: **1 May**; Portugal/Camões Day: **10 June**; Assumption: **15 August**; Republic Day: **5 October**; All Saints' Day: **1 November**; Restoration Day: **1 December**; Immaculate Conception: **8 December**; Christmas Day: **25 December**.

Additionally, there are the moveable feasts of Carnival and Good Friday, as well as the saints' days in June (see *Calendar of Special Events*).

ACCOMMODATION

Lisbon's hotels are graded from 5-star luxury to 2-star modest, followed by a range of establishments calling themselves *albergaria*, *pensão* or *residencial* – of which the 4-star establishments are very agreeable indeed. Virtually all include continental breakfast in the room charge; all top hotels and a few of the more modest establishments have a restaurant serving lunch and dinner. Menus are broadly international, with a few Portuguese dishes included.

If you arrive without a booking, Turismo in the Restauradores will help you find somewhere to stay. Prices vary enormously according to the grade of the accommodation and the season – highest in July and August and cheapest in winter. What follows is a choice of good accomodation across the range. If you are dialling from outside Lisbon dial 01 before the number given.

Five-star Hotels

(over 30,000$oo for a double)

HOTEL DA LAPA
Rua Pau de Bandeira, 4, 1200 Lisbon
Tel: 395 00 05, Fax: 395 06 65
New luxury hotel in Lisbon's classiest neighbourhood to the west of Bairro Alto. Of the hotels recently opened in Lisbon,

this has the best address – though, for drivers, streets are narrow and hard to negotiate.

HOTEL RITZ INTER-CONTINENTAL
Rua Rodrigo da Fonseca, 88, 1070 Lisbon
Tel: 383 20 20, Fax: 357 94 61
Old-established favourite for top money. Half the rooms – all with balconies – overlook the Parque Eduardo VII. First-class restaurants.

HOTEL MERIDIEN
Rua Castilho, 149, 1070 Lisbon
Tel: 383 09 00, Fax: 383 32 31
French-owned and glossily modern. Neighbour of the Ritz on the park. Imaginative food.

HOTEL AVENIDA PALACE
Rua 1 Dezembro, 123, 1200 Lisbon
Tel: 346 01 51, Fax: 342 28 84
100-year-old hotel beside the Rossio with views up the Avenida da Liberdade. Salazar, it's said, had a suite with a secret passage.

HOTEL TIVOLI
Avenida da Liberdade, 175, 1250 Lisbon
Tel: 353 01 81, Fax: 357 94 61
Centrally located on the Avenida da Liberdade, with a big lobby-cum-lounge; there's also a tennis court and a swimming pool in a tree-shaded garden.

Four-star Hotels
(over 15,000$00 for a double)

HOTEL TIVOLI JARDIM
Rua Julio César Machado, 7
1250 Lisbon
Tel: 353 99 71, Fax: 355 65 66
Tucked diagonally behind the Hotel Tivoli, with a parking forecourt. Guests are entitles to use the Tivoli garden, pool, and tennis court.

HOTEL PRINCIPE REAL
Rua da Alegria, 53
1250 Lisbon
Tel: 346 01 16, Fax: 342 21 04
Quiet and cosy hotel (Americans love it) a short way above the Avenida. Pleasant top-floor restaurant.

Three-star Hotels
(15,000$00 for a double)

HOTEL BOTANICO
Rua Mãe de Agua, 16–20, 1250 Lisbon
Tel: 342 03 92; Fax: 342 01 25
An unassuming and pleasant hotel near the botanical gardens. No restaurant.

HOTEL EDUARDO VII
Avenida Fontes Pereira de Melo, 121, 1050 Lisbon
Tel: 353 01 41, Fax: 353 38 79
Above a busy street close to the Praça Marquês de Pombal. It's dated outside but comfortable inside, with a good top-floor restaurant.

HOTEL VENEZA
Avenida da Liberdade, 189, 1250 Lisbon
Tel: 352 26 18, Fax: 352 66 78
New neighbour to the big Tivoli. A 19th-century townhouse gracefully converted, with balconied rooms. No restaurant but serves breakfast.

Two-star Hotels
In central Lisbon (around 10,000$00 for a double)

PENSÃO BORGES
Rua Garret, 108, 1200 Lisbon
Tel: 346 19 51
Small, friendly, and right on the Chiado.

HOTEL INTERNACIONAL
Rua da Betesga, 3, 1100 Lisbon
Tel: 346 64 01, Fax: 347 86 35
Gleaming paint has given this *belle époque*

Typical lounge

building a handsome icing-sugar coating. Old world charm on the Rossio.

Below I recommend two four-star *albergarias*, delightful neighbourhood accommodation full of character, found outside the city centre (15,000$00–21,000$00 for a double).

ALBERGARIA SENHORA DO MONTE
Calçada do Monte, 39
1170 Lisbon
Tel: 886 60 02, Fax: 877 77 83
On a Graça hilltop with a stunning view from every room across to São Jorge castle and the Tejo and down to Alfama. Very comfortable, with rooftop bar and light meals.

YORK HOUSE RESIDENCIA
Rua das Janelas Verdes, 32
1200 Lisbon
Tel: 396 25 44, Fax: 397 27 93
Graham Greene stayed here, enjoying, like many other Englishmen before and since, the old building and courtyard garden. (The Museum of Ancient Art is on the same street.) Unusually for a *residência*, it has a restaurant, and an annexe, Residência Inglesa, in a townhouse down the street.

SPORT

Lisbon, like all Portugal, is crazy about football. The newspapers will tell you when/where major matches are held, but all top matches are televised.

If you fancy a game of **golf**, you can play on several out-of-town courses. Among them:

Crowded Cascais

GOLF ESTORIL SOL
Tel: 923 24 61
Guests at the Estoril Sol hotel can play on the hotel's own 9-hole course for 2,500$00 a day, or for 4,700$00 at **Quinta da Marinha**.

ESTORIL GOLF CLUB
Tel: 468 01 76
18 holes (+9/7); green fees 6,000$00 a day (7.30am–8pm); Saturday, Sunday and holidays are for members only.

QUINTA DA MARINHA GOLF CLUB
Tel: 486 98 91
18 holes designed by Robert Trent Jones; weekday green fees 6,000$00, weekends 7,500$00. Open 7am–sundown.

PENHA LONGA CLUB
Tel: 924 04 20
18 holes and another challenging Robert Trent Jones design. Green fees are 8,000$00 weekdays (7.30am–9pm), 12,000$00 weekends (6.30am–9pm); winter 8am–8pm.

Horse-riding can be arranged with the **Centro Hipico da Marinha** (tel: 486 9084). A 45-minute ride costs 3,000$00, 1½ hours 6,000$00, half a day 10,000$00. For 1,000$00 an hour you can ride with an instructor at **Hipódromo do Lumar** in Lumiar (tel: 759 40 70).

Possibilities for **tennis** include: the **Clube Internacional de Futebol** in Restelo (tel: 301 47 67), for 700$00 an hour per person; the **Clube Internacional de Tenis** in Campolide (tel: 388 20 84), for 700$00 an hour per person; the **Clube Tenis de Monsanto** (tel: 364 87 41) for 650$00 an hour. In the Estoril and Cascais area are the pricier **Estoril Tennis Club** (tel: 468 16 75) at 1,250$00 an hour; the **Country Club de Cascais** (tel: 483 93 01) 950$00 per person per hour; and the **Quinta da Marinha** (tel: 486 96 90) at 800$00 per person per hour.

You can play **squash** at the **Soleil Health Club** (tel: 388 12 55) centrally located in the **Amoreiras** complex, for 2,200$00 an hour. The Soleil Health Club also offers a pool, sauna, massage and gym. To use the gym costs 1,000$00, or 1,500$00 with an instructor.

Take a chance

The **swimming pools** in the Sheraton, Tivoli and Alfa hotels are for guests and members only. The pool at the **Hotel Altis** is open to the public 9am–9pm for 1,700$00 a day. There is also the **Restelo Aquaparque** (tel: 301 70 00), which has reduced admission charges on Monday.

HEALTH & EMERGENCIES

You can safely drink Lisbon city water but if you have a stomach that quivers away from home then stick to mineral water. There are several varieties, some *com gás* (sparkling), others *sem gás*. Toilets are often marked *Homens* for men, *Senhoras* for women.

In Lisbon, there is always a **pharmacy** open somewhere. If you can't find one dial 118 (or get someone else to) for the *Farmácias de serviço*. Hospitals are mostly big and chronically overfull, staff overworked and underpaid. Some foreigners head for the British Hospital (tel: 395 50 67), 49 Rua Saraiva de Carvalho.

When you need the police, an ambulance, the fire brigade, dial **115**.

Crime

Lisbon, like every capital city, suffers from petty crime – mainly handbag-snatching

and occasional mugging in dark streets. Alfama's alleys require extra caution. The obvious solution: be sensible, take care, don't carry too much money. Never leave your possessions unattended or visible in a car.

COMMUNICATIONS & NEWS

Post

Most post offices are open 8.30am–6pm. The central Restauradores post office is open 8am–10pm, the airport post office opens 24 hours. Stamps are *selos*: look for the gluepot to ensure they stay stuck. The EU minimum (20g) is 85$00. Post offices can charge by size, too, so avoid extra-long postcards. All post offices have a *poste restante* service. Have your passport handy for identification.

Telephones

The telephone system, once frustrating, is now good. Many hotels have direct dial service, but this is expensive because they add to the basic charge. You'll see numerous telephone boxes around Lisbon, some for cash, many marked Credifone – for credit cards, which you can buy at any post office. You can also call from post offices and pay with cash afterwards. Some neighbourhood shops have metered public telephones. Dialling internationally is straightforward. The international access code is 00. After this, dial the relevant country code: Australia (61); Canada (1); Germany (49); Italy (39); Japan (81); The Netherlands (31); Spain (34); United Kingdom (44); United States (1). If you are using a US phone credit card, first dial the company's access number listed below: AT&T Tel: 05017-1288; MCI Tel: 05017-1234; Sprint Tel: 05017-1877. For any problems, dial 099 for Europe international, 098 for intercontinental and 090 for interurban. For anyone calling in from overseas, the number for Portugal is 351, followed by 1 for Lisbon. Inside Portugal, Lisbon's code is 01.

Media

There's a large Portuguese press. Dailies like *Público* or *Diário de Notícias* have entertainment and what's on columns. A good entertainment and culture weekly is

Sete. International papers are sold at several kiosks, especially in the Restauradores and around the Rossio. Some foreign dailies make it to the racks by evening of the same day; more often they are on sale one day late.

ATTRACTIONS

International trade fairs are held at FIL – Lisbon International Fair on the Tejo waterfront between the city and Belém; a popular fun fair (**Feira Popular**) is permanently on at the fairground along the Avenida da República.

Fish market

LANGUAGE

If you speak Portuguese you can read Spanish and understand most speech. There are also slight similarities with written French. Otherwise Portuguese, which has many zzzhh and nasal sounds, is not easy to follow. Many Portuguese speak a second language, and most have the tolerance and courtesy to help resolve any problem or query. At Turismo and in virtually all hotels and many restaurants you'll find the major European languages fluently spoken. Yet learning just a few words and phrases in Portuguese will enhance your visit.

Essentials

Good morning	*Bom dia*
Good afternoon	*Boa tarde*
Good evening	*Boa tarde/Boa noite*
Goodnight	*Boa noite*
Hello	*Ola*
Goodbye	*Adeus*
Please	*Faz favor*
Thank you	*Obrigado* (from a man)
	Obrigada
	(from a woman)
Many thanks	*Muito obrigado/a*
I don't speak Portuguese	*Não falo portugûes*
I don't understand	*Não compreendo*
Yes/No	*Sim/Não*

Days of the Week

Sunday	*Domingo*
Monday	*Segunda-feira*
Tuesday	*Terça-feira*
Wednesday	*Quarta-feira*
Thursday	*Quinta-feira*
Friday	*Seixta-feira*
Saturday	*Sabado*

Numbers

1	*Um/Uma*	16	*Dezasseis*
2	*Dois/duas*	17	*Dezassete*
3	*Três*	18	*Dezoito*
4	*Quatro*	19	*Dezanove*
5	*Cinco*	20	*Vinte*
6	*Seis*	30	*Trinta*
7	*Sete*	40	*Quarenta*
8	*Oito*	50	*Cinquenta*
9	*Nove*	60	*Sessenta*
10	*Dez*	70	*Setenta*
11	*Onze*	80	*Oitenta*
12	*Doze*	90	*Noventa*
13	*Treze*	100	*Cem (Cento)*
14	*Quatorze*	200	*Duzentos*
15	*Quinze*	1,000	*Mil*

Questions

Where is...?	*Onde é...?*
When...?	*Quando...?*
How much...?	*Quanto custa?*
Is there...?	*Há...?*
Do you have...?	*Tem...?*
At what time...?	*A que horas...?*
What time is it?	*Que horas são?*
Do you have a room?	*Tem um quarto livre?*

USEFUL ADDRESSES

BRITISH EMBASSY
Rua de São Domingo, 37
Tel: 396 11 91

84

AMERICAN EMBASSY
Avenida das Forças Armadas
Tel: 726 66 00

All embassies are listed in the Lisbon phone book under the word *Embaixada*.

LISBON AIRPORT
Tel: 80 80 44 or 848 11 01

FLIGHT ENQUIRIES
Tel: 80 20 60 or 80 22 62

TAP AIR PORTUGAL
Tel: 848 91 81

Look in the phone book under **Aeroporto de Lisboa** ANA-RP for other airlines.

TOURISM/TURISMO
at the central Palácio Foz in Praça dos Restauradores
Tel: 346 33 14 or 346 36 58

FURTHER READING

Guide Books

Insight Guide: Portugal and *Insight City Guide: Lisbon* (both APA Publications) are comprehensive guides that include in-depth essays on culture by local journalists and writers.

Travel/History/Society

Popular reading is Rose Macaulay's *They Went to Portugal* (Penguin, 1985) on the adventures of notable British travellers across the years. For an overall picture there's my own *The Portuguese: The Land and the People* by Marion Kaplan (Penguin, 1992). You should find books in translation by such superb Portuguese writers as the modern José Saramago or the 19th-century Eça de Queiroz. Portugal's greatest epic is *The Lusiads* by Luís de Camões, translated into English by William C. Atkinson (Penguin, 1952).

Food and Wine

On Portuguese cooking there is the big, illustrated *Traditional Portuguese Cookery* by Maria de Lourdes Modesto (Verbo, in English, too), *The Food of Portugal* by Jean Anderson (Robert Hale, 1986) and *Portuguese Cookery* by Ursula Bourne (Penguin). Books on wine include *Portugal's Wines and Wine Makers* by Richard Mayson (Ebury) and *The Englishman's Wine* – lively reading on port – by Sarah Bradford (Macmillan, 1969).

Lisbon bookshops, especially in the Rua do Carmo, the Chiado, Amoreiras, also have a large range of books on other themes pertinent to the city.

Passing time in Alfama

Index

Museu Militar 35–6
Museu Nacional de Arqueologia e
Etnologia 38
Museu Nacional de Arte Antiga 13, 44–5
Museu Nacional do Azulejo 34
Museu Nacional dos Coches 39
Museum of Decorative Arts of the
Fundação Ricardo Espírito Santo 23
music 33, 61, 72

N, O

'Namban' screens 13, 44, 45
National Pantheon of Santa Engrácia 24
newspapers 83–4
nightlife 32, 71–3
Noites de Queluz 43
de Oliveira, Vicente 42
opera 72
Oporto 43
Ourique 11
'Outra Banda' 57, 58

P

palaces 29, 39, 40, 42–3, 44, 45, 49, 50,
60, 61, 62
Palácio da Fronteira 49
Palácio de Seteais 61–2
Palácio Nacional (Sintra) 60, 61
Palácio Nacional da Ajuda 40
Palácio Pimenta 45
Pena Palace 61, 62
Palmela 11, 65
Paredes, Carlos 72
Parque do Monteiro-Mor 48
Parque Edouardo VII 47
Parque Nacional da Arrábida 64
passports 77
'pastelarias' 24, 39, 50
Pedro IV 42–3
Pereira, Nuno Alvares 30
Pessoa, Fernando 16, 33, 45
petrol 80
pharmacies 83

Philip II (of Spain) 12, 62, 65
police 83
Pombal, Marquês de 14, 17, 27, 40, 44, 59
population 14, 68, 78
port 28, 31, 67, 85
Portinho do Arrábida 64
Porto Brandão 80
post 83
post offices 21, 80, 83
Praça de Comércio 10–1, 16, 21, 26, 57, 80
Praça dos Restauradores 29, 50
Prazeres cemetery 16
public holidays 74, 75, 80
public transport 20, 30, 79 80

Q, R

'queijadas' 60, 63
de Queiroz, Eça 16, 33, 85
Queluz 42–3, 72, 79
Quinta da Marinha 55, 82
Quinta de Bacalhõa 63–4
railways 17, 52, 63, 76, 79
Regaleira 61, 62
religion 78
restaurants 25, 26, 28, 29, 30–1, 32, 36,
40, 43, 54, 57, 63, 68, 69–70, 76
Revolution of 1974 (Young Captains') 15,
17, 30, 74, 77
Robillon, Jean-Baptiste 42
rock music 72, 73
Romans 11–2, 45
Rossio (Praça de Dom Pedro IV) 27, 79
Rossio station 29, 50, 60, 63, 79
Rua Garrett *see* Chiado

S

Salazar, Dr António de Oliveira 14, 15,
17, 24, 78, 81
Santa Apolónia station 36, 76, 79
Santa Justa elevador 20, 30, 80
Santarém 75
Santo António (St Antony of Padua) 22,
74, 75

T

V

W, X, Z

ART & PHOTO CREDITS

Photography	**Marion Kaplan** *and*
Pages 10, 16, 22, 39B, 43, 55, 65B, 73, 75B	**Tony Arruza**
12, 15B, 20, 23, 24, 27,	**Bill Wassman**
30T, 31, 32B, 34, 36T, 40, 41, 51, 52,	
57, 59, 62, 67, 74, 79, 80, 82, 84, 85	
5	**Phil Wood**
13T, 44–46	**Museu Nacional de Arte Antiga, Lisbon**
13B	**Museu da Cidade, Lisbon**
35	**Museu do Azulejo, Lisbon**
Handwriting	**V. Barl**
Cover Design	**Klaus Geisler**
Cartography	**Berndtson & Berndtson**